The
CORNBREAD
Book

The CORNBREAD Book

A LOVE STORY with RECIPES

JEREMY JACKSON

WM

WILLIAM MORROW
An Imprint of HarperCollinsPublishers

HarperCollins books may be purchased for educational, business, or sales promotional use. For information please write: Special Markets Department, HarperCollins Publishers Inc., 10 East 53rd Street, New York, NY 10022.

FIRST EDITION

Designed by Nicola Ferguson

Printed on acid-free paper

Library of Congress Cataloging-in-Publication Data
Jackson, Jeremy, 1973–
The cornbread book : a love story with recipes / Jeremy Jackson.—1st ed.
p.   cm.
Includes bibliographical references and index.
ISBN 0-06-009679-9
1. Cornbread.   I. Title.
TX770.C64 J33 2003
641.8'15—dc21   2002068466

03 04 05 06 07 WBC/QW 10 9 8 7 6 5 4 3 2 1

In memory of my grandmothers—
cooks and storytellers

CORNTENTS

ACKNOWLEDGMENTS

First off I want to thank me. I want to thank me for coming up with the idea for this book, and then writing the proposal, and then developing all the recipes, and then testing the recipes over and over until my eyes were a lovely cornmeal hue. I, after all, had to put up with nightmares about cornbread. Remember the nightmare where it rained cornbread? And also the one where I woke up one morning after a night of excessive drink only to find myself in bed with a strange cornbread whose name I couldn't remember? (I later discovered that it was Zaletti, page 74.) But the worst nightmare of all was when I dreamed that I got a letter that looked like it was a check from someone, but when I opened the envelope a cornbread jumped out and challenged me both physically and verbally.

I also want to thank the various and sundry grackles, starlings, squirrels, chipmunks, raccoons, crows, gnats, flies, and wacky dogs for eating all my failed and/or overflowing cornbread from atop my backyard compost pile. Your service and kindness will not be forgotten.

I thank my agent, David Dunton, for not laughing at me when I first told him my idea for this book.

And I thank my editor, the fantabulous Harriet Bell, for helping me make a great book and also sending me free cookbooks.

In my research, I benefited greatly from access to the Chef Louis Szathmáry II Collection of Culinary Arts in the Special Collections Department of the University of Iowa Libraries.

Most of all I thank my mother, whose commonsense cookery is not only the foundation of my own half-cocked kitchen tomfoolery but who helped me through all stages of this book with inspiration, advice, dishwashing, testing, and excessive enthusiasm.

Acknowledgments

"You tell me whar a man gits his corn pone, en I'll tell you what his 'pinions is."

—*Mark Twain, "Corn-pone Opinions"*

INTRODUCTION

The first thing I'm going to do with this book is make cornbread one word, once and for all. It deserves that much. After all, pancake is one word. So is doorknob. And telemarketer. Telemarketer! Though a few cookbooks and dictionaries do use cornbread as a single word, they are a lonely minority. I won't be satisfied until Merriam-Webster takes note.

The second thing I want to do with this book is to have cornbread named the official bread of the United States of America. It should also be the *unofficial* bread. For example, it should be on all fast food menus. And presidents should choke on cornbread, not pretzels. Also, all newly sworn-in citizens should receive a free piece of cornbread with a little toothpick American flag in it. And when you go to vote, you should get a piece of cornbread as a reward. And when you lick the back of a stamp, it should taste like cornbread, with or without butter, your choice.

My third goal is to find a wife.

My fourth goal is to expand our concept of what cornbread is. Why should the most boring and rubber-esque slab of yellow cornbread we had served to us at some truck stop in South Dakota lay any more claim to the name cornbread, say, than the classic New England anadama bread, or a crusty focaccia made with flour milled from popped popcorn, or cookies with cornmeal in them?

Lookit, I'm tired of being bullied by those self-absorbed biscuit aficionados, and I don't care what the Pan-American Pancake Association says: cornbread, and *only* cornbread, is *the* American bread. Lewis and Clark ate cornbread on their way to the Oregon coast. Thoreau baked cornmeal-rye ash cakes on the shore of Walden Pond. Of course, the original Americans had been making cornbreads long before Europeans appeared and started mucking everything up. But for the purposes of this book, that's where the story of modern cornbread begins: at the intersection of Native American and European culture. This book features breads that are the product of the marriage of corn and wheat.

What, perhaps you're wondering, is my story? Or, more precisely, what's my *damage?* Well, I suppose I was doomed at an early age. Perhaps my mother ate too much cornbread while I was in the womb. Perhaps it can all be traced to the fact that I am the product of my father's family, who grew corn for a living, and my mother's family, who ate corn to live.

But more precisely, I think the trouble can be traced back to my infancy, when the dew was still fresh upon my brow and I moved about the world clad only in a warm pair of red "footie" pajamas. When I was just a toddler, we suffered a wickedly cold winter in Missouri, and our drafty and uninsulated farmhouse was warmed by only two space heaters and a strip heater. The days were so cold I wasn't allowed to play outside, so to satisfy my need for grime and grit my mother took a shallow pan and filled it with a gallon of cornmeal. This was my sandbox, or, more accurately, my cornmeal-box. Daily I would climb up onto the kitchen table—often climbing right into the pan itself—and drive my assorted toy trucks and land movers though the yellow meal. I regularly managed to dust my entire self in cornmeal, as well as part of the kitchen. And if some of the cornmeal got in my mouth, it was inoffensive, unlike sand. When the play was over, my mother would gather up the cornmeal—a process which surely involved a whisk broom, and maybe even a procedure by which I was suspended by the heels of my feet and shaken gently—and pour it back into its gallon jar. So we had two big jars of cornmeal that winter, one labeled "eat" and one labeled "play." Perhaps this is why, to this day, when it comes to cornmeal and cornbread, I associate eating with playing and playing with eating. And, by my calculations, the marriage of playing and eating is cooking. Even now, if I cook some cornbread without managing to fling a bit of cornmeal onto the floor or wall or into my hair, it's not an entirely satisfying experience.

And therefore, in the same manner that the infant Achilles was dipped into the waters of the River Styx to make him invulnerable to injury, I, in my early age, was thoroughly and repeatedly dusted and encrusted with cornmeal. This cornmealification, if you will, unfortunately did not make me invulnerable to pinpricks, small arms fire, or cavities. But it did, I think, create a bond between myself and cornmeal, which naturally let me see the wonderful possibilities, potentialities, and promises of cornbread.

See, cornbread and I have an *understanding*.

I believe in cornbread.

Cornbread, one word.

A Pithy and Perfunctory History of Cornbread in These United States

W hat, as the academics say, is the *deal* with cornbread? In what manner and in what age did humankind first bake corn into loaves or cakes of bread, and what did they put on the bread? Did they put butter on it or no? Was this before butter was invented? Had cows even been invented? Or did these people eat their cornbread plain, a.k.a. "straight up"? Who were these people, and where are they today? If there were a Cornbread Museum and Hall of Fame, who would be honored therein? What kind of colorful dioramas would be on display there? And what would be for sale in the museum's gift shop? Could I get a cornbread key fob? A cornbread shot glass?

All very good questions.

The history of cornbread, though, like that of so many

foods and also that fake plastic "grass" that you put in Easter baskets, is largely shrouded in mystery. Cornbread, after all, is a bread of the people, for the people, and by the people. It's also to the people, at the people, on the people, in the people, nearby the people, around the people, with the people, through the people, and almost any other preposition you can think of. And most of these people didn't read, write, or take the *New York Times,* and therefore the story of their food is largely undocumented. But we must do what we can to unshroud the mystery.

Well, I propose that it all started with corn. Picture this: at some point, about 7,000 years ago, some mopey bloke was slumping by his fire somewhere in the highlands of southern Mexico when the dried seed of a long stalk of grass leaning over the fire exploded and jumped straight toward the poor man and hit him squarely in the forehead. This fellow, in defense, bit into the exploded seed and discovered that it was exceptionally edible, even though it did leave a thin bit of hull wedged securely between two of his molars for six days, which even flossing did not dislodge. Popcorn had been discovered, and, at the same time, so had corn.

Many archeo-botanists do think that popcorn was a likely way that corn was discovered. And once the wild grass was cultivated, it became the stable agricultural base that allowed for the creation of complex civilizations such as those of the Aztec and Maya. Over the centuries, new strains of corn allowed it to be grown in a variety of climates in North and South America, and the people of those continents began baking tortillas and parched corn cakes and so forth. It was the first great age of cornbread cookery. A fine time was had by all.

Meanwhile, back in Europe, everyone wanted gold. I guess they wanted gold to make watches and dobby earrings and nice fountain pens, not to mention bowling trophies, cell phones (there's gold in there, isn't there?), and that crazy liqueur that has gold flakes in it. And the so-called New World was supposedly piled high with gold, so off went the Europeans on a good old-fashioned gold hunt. Little did they suspect that the gold they would find was not of the precious metal sort, of course, but of the corn sort, which eventually would prove to be more useful and precious than all the gold in the world put together, plus silver.

Now, we all know that Europeans are slow to learn and pig-headed. They didn't much care for the wide variety of Native American cornbread cookery that they encountered. They wanted corn to be like their staple grain, wheat. But corn is not like wheat, and wheat is not like corn, and never the twain shall meet. (Or, shall they?) Corn, after all, is both a vegetable and a grain. Wheat converts sugar into starch; but corn converts starch into sugar. And almost any attempt to substitute cornmeal wholly for wheat flour will fail miserably, partly because corn lacks the gluten that allows wheat dough to rise. But because corn was well suited to North America, and wheat was more difficult to grow there, the European settlers were forced to come to terms with this new grain.

Though Columbus and other early explorers had taken note of corn and helped transport its seeds across the globe, Thomas Hariot, who left the ill-fated settlement at Roanoke

Island before it vanished, made what might be the first mention of corn as a basis for a bread in 1588. In describing corn, he wrote that "the graine is about the bignesse of our ordinary English peaze and not much different in form and shape: but of divers colours: some white, some red, some yellow, and some blew. All of them yeeld a very white and sweete flowre: beeing used according to his kinde it maketh a very good bread." But cornbread, it seems, wasn't powerful enough to save Roanoke from failure. This is a powerful lesson: even cornbread has its limits.

Hariot and the other early settlers had learned the cornbread techniques of the natives, but it's difficult to say when the Europeans first created their own style of cornbread by mixing corn with wheat. In the 1630s, Captain John Smith clearly stated that the Virginian settlers had "plentie" of bread, made from wheat, corn, and rye. But were they mixing these grains together? The settlers at Plymouth, meanwhile, were busy stealing the seed corn of the Indians, which they'd found buried in the ground. But they, too, quickly learned from the natives how to make breads from corn. Lo and behold, cornbread was on the menu at the first Thanksgiving. But was there wheat in it? Probably not.

What all the early settlers in North America likely learned from the native populations was how to make corn "pone," which in the various native languages is *oppone, apan, suppawn,* etc. Captain Smith mentions pones as early as 1612. The indigenous pones were probably thin cakes baked in front of the fire or actually in the ashes of the fire, and, of course, they didn't originally have any wheat in them. But to Europe-

The Cornbread Book

ans these pones probably seemed a bit dense. They didn't have any leavening, after all, and they probably didn't have any shortening. All they contained, most likely, was cornmeal, water, and maybe salt. One Dutch visitor to Plymouth called the pones "good but heavy." That's putting it nicely.

Like pones, most early cornbreads adopted by the settlers were probably variations on native breads. The ash cake was baked in the coals of the fire. The johnnycake got its name either from "journey cake"—a long-keeping bread for traveling—or perhaps "Shawnee cake," after one tribe who made such bread. In 1705, Robert Beverly noted that the bread served in "Gentlemen's Houses" was usually made from wheat, but that "some rather choose the Pone, which is the bread made of Indian Meal." In 1737, in his *Natural History of Virginia*, William Byrd wrote that the Indians baked their cornbreads "either in Cakes before the Fire, or in Loaves on a warm Hearth, covering the Loaf first with Leaves, then with warm Ashes, and afterwards with Coals over all."

It's fair to say that in the eyes of the European settlers, the cornbreads of America had from the start been considered a "lesser" bread, inferior to wheat breads. When he was a child, Abraham Lincoln's family ate corn dodgers six days a week, but on Sunday, the sabbath day, they ate wheat bread, a luxury. And Josh Billings, the late-1800s humorist, wrote this damning complaint about the most basic of cornbreads, the corn dodger:

> Injun meal iz made out ov korn, and korn dodgers iz made out ov injun meal, and korn dodgers are the tuffest chunks, ov the bread purswashun, known tew man.

Korn dodgers are made out ov water, with injun meal mixt into it, and then baked on a hard board, in the presence ov a hot fire.

When yu kant drive a 10 penny nail into them, with a sledge hammer, they are sed, bi good judges, to be well done, and are reddy tew be chawed upon.

They will keep 5 years, in a damp place, and not gro tender, and a dog hit with one of them will yell for a week, and then crawl under the barn, and mutter for two days more.

I hav knawed two hours miself on one side of a korn dodger without produsing enny result, and i think i could starve to death twice before i could seduce a korn dodger.

They git the name *dodger* from the immegaite necessity ov dodgeing, if one iz hove horizontally at yu in anger.

It iz far better tew be smote bi a 3 year old steer, than a korn dodger, that iz only three hours old.

If nothing else, Billings's rant is a lesson that most cornbreads are best eaten hot out of the oven; they don't improve with age.

Even the ragamuffin Huckleberry Finn expressed disdain for "low-down corn-pone." Still, Twain himself valued the humble cornbreads of his youth, even though his fame and wealth allowed him to travel and sample the cuisines of the world. While traveling in Italy he grew so tired of the food there that he made a list of the dishes he wanted to greet him upon his return to America. The list included both pone and hoecake.

Benjamin Franklin was an early defender of the rustic cornbreads of North America. When Americans were threatening to boycott tea in protest of the Stamp Act, an anonymous letter in the London *Gazetteer* claimed that "the Americans, should they resolve to drink no more tea, can by no means keep that Resolution, their Indian corn not affording an agreeable or easy digestible breakfast." Franklin countered with a letter of his own, defending an array of corn cookery, and claiming that "johny or hoecake, hot from the fire, is better than a Yorkshire muffin."

And though cornbread's lack of sophistication and association with all things lowly were reasons it was held in disdain, others reveled in its simplicity and wholesomeness. In "Economy," the opening chapter of *Walden,* Henry David Thoreau described his cornbread experiments:

> Bread I at first made of pure Indian meal and salt, genuine hoe-cakes, which I baked before my fire out of doors on a shingle or the end of a stick of timber sawed off in building my house; but it was wont to get smoked and to have a piny flavor. I tried flour also; but have at last found a mixture of rye and Indian meal most convenient and agreeable. In cold weather it was no little amusement to bake several small loaves of this in succession, tending and turning them as carefully as an

Egyptian his hatching eggs. They were a real cereal fruit which I ripened, and they had to my senses a fragrance like that of other noble fruits . . .

He went on to say that he didn't think yeast improved the cornbread at all. Of course it didn't! The combination of cornmeal and rye flour would not produce enough gluten to make the dough rise significantly. So he stopped using yeast, or any other leavening. "I am glad," he wrote, "to escape the trivialness of carrying a bottle-full [of yeast] in my pocket, which would sometimes pop and discharge its contents to my discomfiture."

Thoreau was pleased to have formulated a simple bread that didn't require the luxuries of yeast and wheat flour, and he saw it as a means towards a more self-reliant life:

> Every New Englander might easily raise all his own breadstuffs in this land of rye and Indian corn, and not depend on distant and fluctuating markets for them. Yet so far are we from simplicity and independence that, in Concord, fresh and sweet meal is rarely sold in shops. . . . For the most part the farmer gives to his cattle and hogs the grain of his own producing, and buys flour, which is at least no more wholesome, at a greater cost, at the store.

He was right, of course, that corn in particular was a more economical provision than wheat flour. Wheat, after all, did not become cheap in America until the Midwest was widely settled, and even the pioneers in those lands relied on corn to sustain them until wheat could be established. All Americans of humble means relied on corn, from pioneers and settlers to hillbillies and slaves. Slave owners supplied cornmeal to their slaves because it was cheap. The slaves' reliance on corn and cornbread is one reason why the southern United States has such a strong tradition of cornbread cookery.

Despite cornbread's role in the the success of the early European settlements in America, it took 300 years from Columbus's first encounter with corn before cornbread appeared in a cookbook. In 1796, Amelia Simmons published *American Cookery*, generally considered the first American cookbook. On its title page the book claimed to be "adapted to this country." And indeed it had five recipes with cornmeal in them: three Indian puddings, one for "Johny Cake or Hoe Cake," and one for Indian Slapjacks.

Despite the continued reliance on simple cornbreads, the nineteenth century also saw the blossoming of "modern" cornbreads, those cornbreads made with wheat flour, milk, shortening, sugar, eggs, and leavening—all of which were relative luxuries, and all of which produced a softer and richer bread that was more palatable to more people. American recipe books appeared in great numbers in the 1800s, and many of them included multiple recipes for these new rich cornbreads. Also more yeast breads that incorporated cornmeal were appearing. Adding a proportion of cornmeal to a wheat flour yeast bread was a good way of economizing while still producing a nicely risen loaf. Lydia Child, in her 1829 book *The American Frugal Housewife*, gives the recipe for what is often referred to as "thirded bread," a yeast loaf made of equal parts wheat flour, rye flour, and cornmeal. (My version is on page 102.) "Rye 'n' Injun" was a similar yeast bread that originated in colonial New England. The ubiquitous anadama bread supposedly came from New England, too, sometime in the 1800s.

By the twentieth century, of course, wheat was available widely and cheaply—though still not as cheaply as cornmeal—and for the first time in American history, wheat bread became the most common bread. And the industrialization of food processing was not kind to cornmeal. Modern millers began degerminating their cornmeal. The excuse for this—or at least what they told consumers—was that degerminated cornmeal kept fresh much longer. That much is true. But the real reason for degerminating cornmeal, even today, is that the miller can then sell the corn germ for corn oil, which is more lucrative than selling whole-grain cornmeal. And when you degerminate the corn, you also remove much of the flavor. Modern mega-millers think of cornmeal as a by-product of corn oil, gluten meal (a livestock feed), fuel ethanol, and corn syrup manufacturing.

Still, cornbread had its shining moments in the twentieth century. During World War I, Congress urged Americans to eat cornmeal in some form every day, so that all available wheat could be sent to the Allied forces overseas. The agricultural markets in many parts of Europe were in shambles, of course, and America could help make up for the loss. In the introduction to a 1917 revised edition of *American Indian Corn (Maize): A Cheap, Wholesome, and Nutritious Food*, 150

Ways to Prepare and Cook It, Jeanette Young Norton penned these immortal words: "Millions of people in America are earnestly seeking a way to 'do their bit' toward winning the war. Here is a simple solution of the problem: EAT CORN BREAD!"

Amen.

That book, which was reprinted solely for the purpose of encouraging cornmeal consumption for the war effort, included a variety of corn recipes, including such wartime recipes as "1917 War Coffee"—toasted cornmeal coated with molasses that is meant to be a substitute for ground coffee—and "Government War Bread 1917"—a yeast bread remarkably similar to thirded bread.

Corn also helped feed the nation during the Great Depression. For corn is a hardy crop, and it rarely fails completely.

World War II saw another revival of cornmeal cookery, including the remarkable use of "popcorn flour" in breads. When President Truman ordered bakers to use less wheat flour, the H. Piper Company, then a major retail bakery in Chicago, sought alternatives and found that popped popcorn that was milled into a "flour" was an excellent way to stretch their wheat flour supply. In fact, many people thought that the combination of 25 percent popcorn flour and 75 percent wheat flour created a bread that was superior to one made with wheat flour alone. The popcorn gave the bread "a higher protein content, a richer color, and a much better taste," as well as giving the bread a longer shelf life. The popcorn breads were so successful that H. Piper kept them even after the war ended. But a poor popcorn crop in 1947 sent popcorn prices soaring, and H. Piper dropped their popcorn bread. The use of popcorn flour has largely disappeared, though for this book I developed three recipes that use it, and I found that it does indeed make an excellent yeast bread. Some baker out there with more yeast bread experience than I have should write a whole book about popcorn flour.

Since World War II, cornbread has been a minor player in the world of breads. Sure, it has its occasional moments of fame, such as the craze for blue cornbread. The continued "Balkanization" of cornbreads has perhaps placed too much emphasis on the idea that certain cornbreads are or aren't "authentic." Any cornbread that has corn in it is authentic, as far as I'm concerned. And though southern cuisine still celebrates cornbread much more than any other region, even southerners are consumed by the idea that only white cornmeal can make "real" cornbread. Meanwhile, most people seem to get their cornbread recipe off the back of the Quaker cornmeal box (even Julia Child admits as much) or out of the Jiffy box. What's next? Cornbread without cornmeal in it? Liquid cornbread? Cornbread-flavored coffee at Starbucks?

Is the time of cornbread past? Is this the twilight of cornmeal cookery in America? Will we allow ourselves to be fooled into thinking that degerminated cornmeal is the way cornmeal should taste? Will we limit ourselves to making cornbread only with cornmeal, ignoring breads with sweet corn, hominy, and popcorn flour?

Or is cornbread once again ascendant? Is the bread that built America about to have its second coming? Maybe so.

It's morning in Cornbreadland.

INGREDIENTS

Cornmeal

If I had my druthers, I'd require that all kindergarten classes in the United States teach a unit on cornmeal, followed by increasingly complex lessons in the fourth, eighth, and twelfth grades. Perhaps this would help our country understand that cornmeal comes in many different forms and flavors. Just like flour, coffee beans, wine, and even salt, there are a variety of cornmeals, which vary in color, grind, breed of corn, milling process, and freshness. Unfortunately, the cornmeal business in America is stunningly tight-lipped about its own product. Retail packages of cornmeal almost never specify what kind of corn they are made from, or even how recently they were milled.

Though in my next book, *Granulated Gold: A Mind-Numbing and Immense History and/or Celebration of Cornmeal,*

Hominy Grits, and Cracked Corn (which is told in verse), I may have time to appropriately exhaust this subject, for our purposes here, I offer the following guidance.

First, if nothing else, we need to understand the two basic categories of cornmeal: whole-grain (often called "stone ground") and degerminated.

Whole-grain cornmeal is made from dried kernels of corn that have not been altered. Almost always, whole-grain cornmeal is "stone ground," which means it is milled between stones, the old-fashioned way of doing it. The stone-grinding process mills the corn at a lower temperature, avoiding the danger of "scorching" the corn and altering its flavor. Whole-grain cornmeal is not uniform in shape—it contains small pieces (a.k.a. "dust") and larger pieces, and everything in between. It is mottled in color. The good news about whole-grain cornmeal is that when it's fresh, it is flavorful and homey and individual. A fresh whole-grain cornmeal has a fantastic nutty flavor with a nice grassy kick. But these flavors can vary quite a bit, just as wines made from the same kind of grape can vary. Whole-grain cornmeal is more nutritious, too, than the degerminated variety. The bad news about whole-grain cornmeal is that it spoils if it isn't kept cold. And the even worse news is that hardly any cornmeal manufacturers date-stamp their cornmeal so you can tell how old it is when you buy it. I would never buy whole-grain cornmeal that is more than two months old. I much prefer to buy it earlier than that. (If you're inclined to mill your own corn at home with a hand mill or electric mill, you'll get the freshest cornmeal of all.) And when I get whole-grain cornmeal home, I put it in an airtight bag in the freezer immediately. Frozen, it lasts for months, or perhaps up to two years. (Mine's never around that long.)

Degerminated cornmeal (sometimes called "granulated" cornmeal) is a different beast. Most degerminated cornmeal is ground between steel rollers. By removing the germ, a uniform, shelf-stable product is created. It can generally last for at least a year at room temperature before it goes stale. The germ, though, is rich with oil, nutrients, and flavor, and it is sorely missed. Nonetheless, degerminated cornmeal does make fine cornbread—though not as good as a bread made with fresh whole-grain cornmeal. In some circumstances, degerminated cornmeal's subdued flavor and uniformity make it appealing. In fact, because of its uniformity, neutral flavor, universality, and shelf life, I chose to use degerminated cornmeal (specifically, Quaker yellow) to develop all the recipes in this book. This is not meant as an endorsement of degerminated cornmeal. In most instances, a fresh whole-grain cornmeal will produce a better bread. As you bake the recipes in this book, feel free to use either degerminated or whole-grain cornmeal. Yes, each cornmeal is slightly different in how much water it will absorb, how it bonds with other ingredients, etc., but there's really no way to know the characteristics of an individual cornmeal until you cook with it.

Colors: Yes, cornmeal comes in a variety of colors, from the ubiquitous yellow cornmeal to the white cornmeal preferred in the South. And then there's also blue cornmeal, from the Southwest, and red, purple, black, and pink. Though the vitamin content and nutritional value vary slightly from color to color, the flavors of the cornmeals aren't dramatically different, particularly if you're comparing degerminated cornmeals. For this reason, I don't specify a particular color of cornmeal in my recipes. If you want blue muffins, use blue cornmeal. It's up to you. Knock yourself out. Nonetheless, many southerners swear that only white cornmeal makes proper cornbread. What's my opinion of that? I invoke my right to keep my pie-hole shut in order not to offend anyone.

Most supermarkets nowadays have more than one cornmeal on the shelves. Perhaps most common is Quaker cornmeal, which is a degerminated and enriched cornmeal sold in both yellow and white varieties. It is comparable to Aunt Jemima cornmeal, which is also made by Quaker. There are other brands of degerminated cornmeal, but there isn't a great deal of difference between them.

As for brands of whole-grain cornmeal, you might find brands such as Martha White, Hodgson Mill, Bob's Red Mill, and Arrowhead Mills in your supermarket. They can be quite good, but I worry about their freshness sometimes. How long has it been since they've been milled? You can also find fresh whole-grain cornmeal in a natural foods store or bulk foods store. I'm lucky that my local natural foods coop has bulk organic whole-grain cornmeal that usually tastes quite fresh. It's far cheaper than national brands, too. King Arthur Flour sells a whole-grain organic cornmeal online and via mail order.

Another way to get good whole-grain cornmeal is to patronize one of the small mills that are still in operation in our country. If you're lucky enough to have one in your community, visit them and ask how often they mill their corn. A handful of old-timey mills have websites where you can buy their product. Weisenberger Mill, War Eagle Mill, and Nora Mill Granary are examples. I've listed their Web addresses at the back of the book.

A note: Polenta is simply the Italian name for cornmeal (it's also the name of the cornmeal mush that it makes). But polenta is usually a coarser grind than most cornmeals, and therefore it's not always ideal to substitute polenta for cornmeal.

Corn Flour

In Britain corn flour refers to cornstarch, but here in the States corn flour simply means corn that has been milled to a very fine consistency, like wheat flour. It's useful in recipes where you want the flavor of cornmeal, but a smoother texture.

Some grocery stores do carry corn flour—Bob's Red Mill is a common brand—usually in the little section of what I call hippie flours, like rye flour, potato flour, rice flour, etc. Bulk foods stores often carry corn flour, too. In the Midwest, corn flour is common (and cheap) in the bulk foods stores that are operated by the Amish and Mennonites.

You can also find corn flour online. One corn flour I've used is made by Authentic Foods, and can be bought at www.glutenfreemall.com. Bob's Red Mill also sells their corn flour online.

Though masa harina, used in Mexican cooking, is a corn flour, it's processed with alkali and pre-cooked. I don't recommend substituting it for corn flour.

Popcorn Flour

I've never seen a commercial source for popcorn flour (sometimes called "milled popcorn flour"). It's always easy to make your own anyway, and then you're guaranteed that it's fresh. It's also whole-grain!

To make popcorn flour, first pop your popcorn. I always start with ⅓ cup of popcorn kernels. Doesn't matter which color or size. Don't salt them. My preferred method is to put 2 tablespoons of canola oil and 3 unpopped kernels in a 3- to 4-quart stockpot, cover, and heat over medium-high heat, or slightly lower, until the first kernel pops, then add the ⅓ cup of kernels to the pot and wait. When the kernels begin popping, shake the pot frequently to keep the popped kernels from burning. Allow your popcorn to cool, then, working with one cup at a time, put the popcorn into your blender or food processor and process until the popcorn resembles a very coarse meal, kind of like instant tapioca powder. Use whatever popcorn flour you need and freeze the remainder in an airtight bag. It keeps well.

Flour

I developed all recipes in this book using Gold Medal Unbleached All-Purpose Flour. You can expect similar results with any national brand all-purpose or unbleached all-purpose flour. Though I'm a fan of King Arthur Unbleached All-Purpose Flour, its higher protein content makes it slightly less suitable for some of my recipes. It makes great yeast breads, though, and if you want to try it in my yeast breads, keep in mind to use just slightly less flour than the recipe calls for.

Though "soft" southern flours—like White Lily and Red Band—generally make excellent quick breads, I find unbleached all-purpose flour to be exceptionally versatile.

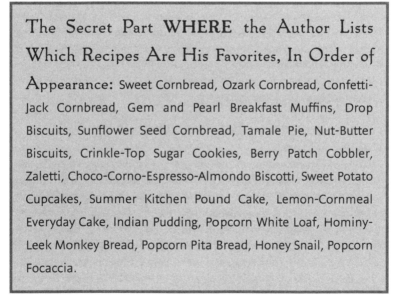

The Secret Part **WHERE** the Author Lists Which Recipes Are His Favorites, In Order of Appearance: Sweet Cornbread, Ozark Cornbread, Confetti-Jack Cornbread, Gem and Pearl Breakfast Muffins, Drop Biscuits, Sunflower Seed Cornbread, Tamale Pie, Nut-Butter Biscuits, Crinkle-Top Sugar Cookies, Berry Patch Cobbler, Zaletti, Choco-Corno-Espresso-Almondo Biscotti, Sweet Potato Cupcakes, Summer Kitchen Pound Cake, Lemon-Cornmeal Everyday Cake, Indian Pudding, Popcorn White Loaf, Hominy-Leek Monkey Bread, Popcorn Pita Bread, Honey Snail, Popcorn Focaccia.

Yeast

I use no other yeast than SAF-Instant "red label," which comes in 500-gram vacuum-packed "bricks." They are more economical than those ¼-ounce packets. Though instant yeast requires no proofing, I wrote a proofing step into all my yeast bread recipes. If you're using instant yeast, you don't have to wait for it to dissolve in the liquid before moving on. Active yeast can be substituted for instant yeast.

EQUIPMENT

One of the splendid things about cornbread is that it isn't particularly finicky about what kind of pan it's baked in. I've had good luck with aluminum, steel, and nonstick bakeware, as long as the pans aren't too thin or flimsy. True, a dark or black pan cooks the crust more quickly than a light-colored or reflective pan, so some caution is required when using such a pan. In particular, I find that dark baking sheets and cookie sheets tend to burn the bottoms of cookies, biscuits, etc. But the choice of bakeware is more a matter of personal preference than anything.

Many people will tell you that good cornbread can only be made in a cast iron skillet. Cast iron cooks the cornbread evenly and thoroughly, especially if the skillet is heated in the oven before the batter is poured in. The addition of oil or shortening to the hot skillet makes for an excellent "fried" crust. If there is a downside to cast iron bakeware, it is its black color, which may brown the crust too quickly. Also, the skillets are heavy, and preheating them before adding the batter is just an accident waiting to happen. I've burned myself more times than I care to count when handling hot iron skillets. Any of the cornbreads in the Basic Cornbreads section of this book can be cooked in a cast iron skillet anywhere from 9 to 12 inches in diameter. A good brand of cast iron cookware is Lodge. It's even better if you inherit a well-seasoned skillet that has been around for years, or even generations.

Cornstick pans, which are cast iron pans with seven to nine corn-ear-shaped grooves, are a favorite way to make cornbread. Again, these pans are often heated before the batter is added, and each groove is usually filled with a little bit of oil or shortening.

You can also make cornbread in muffin pans of any size. Typically, muffins bake faster than a pan of cornbread, so watch them carefully.

You can make a decent cornbread in a glass or porcelain baking dish. But a metal pan usually produces a better crust and a more even "rise." Of course, some of my recipes call for "baking dishes"—Berry Patch Cobbler and Caramel Corncake, for example—and glass dishes are preferred then.

For some of my yeast breads, I call for the use of a baking stone, sometimes called a pizza stone. A baking stone is nothing more than a thin sheet of unglazed ceramic, usually square or round, that you bake your bread directly on. The stone helps bake the bread quickly and evenly, and produces a superior crust, especially when used in combination with some kind of steam introduced into the oven. If you regularly bake yeast breads, especially pizza or rustic loaves, a baking stone is one of the best investments you can make. You can find baking stones in cookware shops and department stores for as little as fifteen dollars. Some people actually buy unglazed tiles at a tile store. They work great, and they're cheap. To use your baking stone, place it on your oven's lowest rack, and allow it to heat in the oven for at least 30 minutes before you put the bread in.

BASIC
CORNBREADS

In which we first encounter the fundamentals of Cornbread.

Herein we learn the formulas and methods of constructing such delectable and comforting breads as the ever-popular Sweet Cornbread and its bold archnemesis, the sugarless and rich-crusted Ozark Cornbread. But wait! Hark! Lo! We also learn that all these simple and unassuming cornbreads will gracefully accept a dazzling variety of additions. Peppers! Cheese! Corn! Sunflower seeds? Yes, sunflower seeds. Read on.

Sweet Cornbread

The cakelike texture of this easy-to-make cornbread is appealing, but it's the sweetness that wins me over time and again. It's a northern-style cornbread in the sense that it has a high ratio of flour, lots of sugar, and sweet milk instead of buttermilk. Northern cornbreads are traditionally made with yellow cornmeal, but that's more an aesthetic choice than anything else. Most of the time when I want cornbread, this is the recipe I go to.

1 cup unbleached all-purpose flour
1 cup cornmeal
5 tablespoons sugar
2 teaspoons baking powder
$\frac{1}{2}$ teaspoon salt
1 cup milk
$\frac{1}{3}$ cup canola oil
1 large egg, slightly beaten

1.   Preheat your oven to 400°F. Grease an 8 × 8- or 9 × 9-inch baking pan with vegetable shortening or nonstick cooking spray.

2.   Sift the dry ingredients into a mixing bowl. Form a well in the mixture and add the milk, oil, and egg. Stir just until everything is combined—there should still be scattered clumps of flour, about the size of baby peas or BBs.

3. Pour the batter into the prepared pan and bake for 24 to 30 minutes, until the cornbread is starting to brown slightly (especially at the edges) and a knife inserted in the middle comes out clean. Serve hot.

Middle-of-the-Road Cornbread: So called because it's not as sweet or rich as Sweet Cornbread. It's the kind of cornbread you hope your daughter will marry someday. Follow the above directions for Sweet Cornbread, but use only 1 to 3 tablespoons of sugar, and only ¼ cup canola oil.

Buttermilk Cornbread

makes 8 or 9 pieces

This moist, full-flavored, buttermilk-based cornbread is similar in nature and spirit to many of the favorite cornbreads of the South, which are usually made with white cornmeal. Often they don't contain any sugar.

> 1 tablespoon plus ¼ cup canola oil
> 1½ cups cornmeal
> ¼ cup plus 2 tablespoons unbleached all-purpose flour (or ½ cup soft southern flour such as White Lily or Red Band)
> 2 teaspoons sugar
> 1 teaspoon salt
> 1 teaspoon baking soda
> 1½ cups buttermilk
> 1 large egg

1.   Preheat your oven all the way to 450°F. When it's reached that temperature, put the 1 tablespoon canola oil into a 9 × 9-inch baking pan or 10½-inch iron skillet and put the pan/skillet into the oven to heat.

2.   Whisk the dry ingredients together until they're well combined and there aren't any lumps of baking soda visible. Separately, whisk the buttermilk, egg, and ¼ cup oil together until they are smooth. Pour the wet ingredients into the dry ingredients, and stir until just combined.

3. Remove the hot pan/skillet from the oven and pour the batter into the pan. The batter will sizzle as it hits the hot oil. Shake the batter into the corners of the pan and then return it quickly to the oven.

4. Bake the cornbread for 18 to 26 minutes, until it's lightly browned. Serve hot.

Creamed Corn Cornbread

makes 9 pieces

This sweet cornbread packs a double corn flavor from cornmeal and canned creamed corn. Many people love corn kernels in their cornbread. You'll get good results with either canned creamed corn or homemade creamed corn.

1 cup unbleached all-purpose flour
1 cup cornmeal
2 teaspoons baking powder
1 teaspoon salt
1 cup creamed corn
1 large egg
¾ cup milk
2 tablespoons honey
2 tablespoons unsalted butter, melted

1.   Preheat your oven to 425°F. Grease an 8 × 8- or 9 × 9-inch baking pan with vegetable shortening or nonstick cooking spray.

2.   Sift the flour, cornmeal, baking powder, and salt into a large bowl. Stir the mixture briefly. Separately, whisk together the creamed corn, egg, milk, honey, and butter until the honey is dissolved.

3.   Add the wet ingredients to the dry ingredients and stir until everything is just combined. Pour the batter into the pan. Bake for 20 to 26 minutes, until golden.

Homemade Creamed Corn: You'll need 3 medium ears of corn, the fresher the better, but with the modern supersweet varieties, you'll get a very good creamed corn even with that corn on the cob you find in your supermarket in February.

Husk, desilk, and wash the ears. Drop the ears into boiling water. Boil for 3 minutes. Remove the ears and transfer them to a bowl or sink full of very cold water. When cool enough to handle, slice off a small piece on one end. Stand the corn on the flat end and slice the kernels off the ears with a knife, into a bowl. The corn will come off in "sheets." Now take the denuded ears of corn and scrape them with your knife blade, squeezing any remaining pulp and liquid from the cob into the same bowl. The result will be a thick corn gruel with a milky liquid oozing about: you've got fresh creamed corn. Collect 1 cup of it for the recipe, then proceed.

Ozark Cornbread

Historically, cornmeal was easier to come by than flour, and also cheaper, so many Americans in all regions of the country subsisted on breads that contained no flour. If you can get fresh, whole-grain cornmeal, this cornbread is the one to make. It's the cornbread I grew up on, which is perhaps why I grew up to be so manly and healthy. My sisters and I prized the crisp corner pieces.

> 2 tablespoons plus ¼ cup canola oil
> 1⅔ cups cornmeal (preferably whole-grain)
> 1 tablespoon baking powder
> 1 teaspoon salt
> 1 cup milk
> 1 large egg

1.   Preheat your oven to 400°F. Put the 2 tablespoons canola oil in an 8 × 8- or 9 × 9-inch baking pan and put the pan in the oven to heat.

2.   Stir together the cornmeal, baking powder, and salt. Add the milk, egg, and the ¼ cup oil and stir until just combined. There should still be small lumps in the batter.

3.   Remove the hot pan from the oven, pour the batter into it, then shake it carefully to spread the batter into the corners. Bake for 22 to 28 minutes, or until firm and just beginning to brown.

Healthier Cornbread

I don't like the name of this cornbread. First, it gives the impression that other cornbreads are unhealthy, which isn't quite true. Second, it just doesn't sound appetizing, when in fact this cornbread is moist, flavorful, crusty, and inviting. If you can get your hands on some freshly milled whole-grain cornmeal, it will make this cornbread even better.

1½ cups cornmeal (preferably whole-grain)
½ cup unbleached all-purpose flour
1 tablespoon sugar
2 teaspoons baking powder
½ teaspoon baking soda
½ teaspoon salt, optional
1 cup (8 ounces) plain fat-free yogurt
2 large egg whites
3 tablespoons olive oil or canola oil

1. Preheat your oven to 400°F. Spray an 8 × 8- or 9 × 9-inch baking pan with cooking spray (or use a nonstick pan).

2. Sift the cornmeal, flour, sugar, baking powder, baking soda, and salt (if desired) into a bowl. Make a well in the middle and add the yogurt, egg whites, and oil. Stir just until everything is combined, then spread the batter into the pan and bake for 20 to 26 minutes, until firm and just beginning to brown.

Cornbread Add-ins and Substitutions

Part of the joy of cornbread is throwing random ingredients into it and seeing what happens. Sweet Cornbread, Buttermilk Cornbread, Creamed Corn Cornbread, Ozark Cornbread, and Healthier Cornbread all accept added ingredients and substitutions nicely. By all means, experiment on your own, create combinations of two or three add-ins, and substitute to your heart's content. Stir them in at the last moment before baking.

Add-ins

Corn kernels, 1 cup, fresh, canned, or frozen

Rice, 1 cup, cooked

Hominy, 1 cup, canned, drained

Garlic, 1 or more cloves, minced

Sun-dried tomatoes, ½ cup, diced

Peppers, 1 or more, diced, seeds removed

Onion, 1, diced

Nuts and seeds, ¼ to 1 cup: poppyseeds, sesame seeds, pumpkin seeds, pine nuts, walnuts, pecans, etc.

Dried fruits and berries, 1 to 1½ cups strawberries, prunes, raisins, currants, dates, figs, cherries, etc.

Cheese, ¾ to 2 cups: almost any variety, shredded, cubed, grated, crumbled, or sliced

Fresh herbs, ¼ cup, minced

Freshly ground black pepper, to taste

Chili powder, 2 tablespoons

Chipotle chile, 2 tablespoons, ground

Red pepper flakes, ½ to 2 teaspoons

Substitutions
Roasted cornmeal for regular cornmeal
Honey, maple syrup, or brown sugar for sugar
Soy milk or goat's milk for milk
Yogurt for buttermilk

Shapes
In addition to baking cornbread in an 8 × 8- or 9 × 9-inch pan, with a single recipe you can make 12 muffins or 14 corn sticks (2 pans of 7). Reduce the baking time by a few minutes.

Three Peppery Cornbreads

One of the popular incarnations of cornbread in recent years is certainly the ubiquitous Southwestern or Tex-Mex cornbread, full of peppers, onions, and other flavors. Here are three of my favorites, but this is the kind of cornbread that begs for improvisation, so try your own combinations. In addition to the kind of things I list here, try adding corn kernels, garlic, red pepper flakes, chili powder, etc.

Here's the blueprint, which is the same for all three of these easy cornbread variations. After your add-in ingredients are ready, prepare your favorite basic cornbread (Middle-of-the-Road Cornbread on page 31 is my favorite vehicle for peppery cornbread). After you've briefly stirred the wet and dry ingredients of the cornbread together, add the peppery ingredients and stir until everything is just combined. Bake according to whichever cornbread recipe you're using.

CONFETTI-JACK CORNBREAD This pairing of bell peppers with Monterey Jack cheese is a surefire crowd pleaser, especially if you combine two or three different colors of peppers. I like to make this with half of a red pepper and half of a green pepper, but it works just as well with one color of pepper.

1 cup bell pepper (about 1 whole pepper), any color, cored, seeded, and chopped
¾ cup (about 3 ounces) grated Monterey Jack cheese, packed

CORNBREAD WITH ROASTED RED PEPPER AND GREEN ONIONS I never serve this to guests because I want it all for myself. For me! I'm a rock star!

1 roasted red bell pepper, peeled, cored, seeded, and
   chopped
4 green onions, diced, white and light green parts only

THE-KIND-OF-PEPPERS-THAT-CAN-MAIM-YOU CORNBREAD
If you have a taste for this kind of thing, it's sublime.

3 to 5 habanero, Jamaican hot, Scotch bonnet, or
   jalapeño peppers, cored, seeded, and chopped
1 small yellow onion, diced

Gem and Pearl Breakfast Muffins

makes 12 muffins

Some will accuse these of being cupcakes in a cunning disguise. I plan to ignore such naysayers, cynics, and out-of-work poets and enjoy my muffins without worrying about semantics. The cream cheese buds that crown these muffins do resemble pearls, but the gems—dabs of jam—are hidden inside. Freeze a whole batch of these for breakfast on the run. In a pinch, call them cupcakes and serve them for dessert. Just don't tell me about it.

> 1 ¼ cups unbleached all-purpose flour
> ½ cup cornmeal
> ½ cup sugar
> 1 tablespoon baking powder
> ½ teaspoon salt
> 1 cup milk
> ½ cup unsalted butter, melted, slightly cooled
> 1 large egg
> Jam or preserves of your choice
> Cream cheese or Neufchâtel cheese (Unfortunately, low-fat versions tend to "melt" while baking, leaving you with a hole in your muffin. I call such muffins "Stolen Pearl Muffins" and they taste great, but don't look very nice.)
> Turbinado sugar for sprinkling, optional

1. Preheat your oven to 375°F. Grease 12 muffin cups with vegetable shortening or nonstick cooking spray or line them with paper.

2. Sift the flour, cornmeal, sugar, baking powder, and salt into a medium bowl. Separately whisk together the milk, butter, and egg. Add the wet ingredients to the dry ingredients and stir quickly until everything is just combined—there should still be some tiny lumps in the batter.

3. Fill each muffin cup one-third full with batter. In the middle of each cup place about 1 teaspoon of jam or preserves. It helps to make a little well in the batter to hold the jam, otherwise it may leak out the sides of the muffin. On the other hand, don't make a well so deep that the jam's actually resting right on the metal of the muffin pan.

4. Fill the muffin cups with the rest of the batter, so that each cup is about two-thirds full. Smooth the batter tops to cover any jam that may be peeking through. Take teaspoon-size balls of cream cheese (a melon ball scoop works well) and push one into the top of each muffin. Don't push them too far—just so they're about half buried. Sprinkle turbinado sugar over the muffin tops, if desired.

5. Bake the muffins for 18 to 22 minutes, until golden and firm.

Berry Muffins: Instead of jam and cream cheese, stir 1 cup fresh or frozen blueberries, strawberries, blackberries, or other berries into the batter.

Cherry-Chocolate Muffins: Instead of jam and cream cheese, stir in ½ cup dried cherries and ½ cup semisweet, bittersweet, or white chocolate chips.

Drop Biscuits

The cornmeal flavor is featured front and center in these crusty biscuits. Drop biscuits are so easy: no fussing with cutting in the shortening, no worries about overhandling the batter. You can have these in the oven in three minutes. Honestly. In fact, the batter will be ready before your oven is heated to the right temperature.

½ cup unbleached all-purpose flour
½ cup cornmeal
¼ plus ⅛ teaspoon salt
¼ teaspoon baking powder
¼ teaspoon baking soda
½ cup buttermilk
3 tablespoons unsalted butter, softened

1.   Preheat your oven to 400°F.

2.   Sift the dry ingredients together into a bowl, then stir in the buttermilk and butter. Use a large spoon to plop the batter onto an ungreased baking sheet. Make 8 to 12 biscuit-size plops.

3.   Bake for 14 to 20 minutes, until lightly browned on the bottom. Serve hot.

Dumpling Topping: Nothing is as homey as a steaming bowl of stew or chili topped with a crusty dumpling. To be honest, I like to make the above drop biscuits and then simply place them on top of the stew before serving—a kind of faux dumplings. But for real dumplings, plop the above batter right on top of the stew as it simmers on the stovetop, making sure it rests on something solid, draining some of the liquid away if there's too much. Cover the stew and let it simmer until the dumplings are done, 12 to 20 minutes.

Sunflower Seed Cornbread

makes 9 pieces

This is really just a variation of Sweet Cornbread, but it's different enough (and good enough) to warrant its own recipe. If you've never had biscuits or cornbread made with sunflower seed meal, you're missing a great treat. To make sunflower seed meal yourself, simply grind raw unsalted sunflower seeds in your blender or food processor until they resemble coarse cornmeal.

²/₃ cup cornmeal

²/₃ cup unbleached all-purpose flour

²/₃ cup sunflower seed meal (made from about
    ²/₃ cup raw seeds)

1 tablespoon baking powder

1 tablespoon sugar

1 teaspoon salt

1 cup milk

¹/₃ cup canola oil

1 large egg, slightly beaten

1. Preheat your oven to 400°F. Lightly grease a 9 × 9-inch baking pan with vegetable shortening or nonstick cooking spray.

2. Stir the dry ingredients together in a medium bowl until they are thoroughly mixed. Add the milk, oil, and egg, and stir until everything is just combined.

3. Pour the batter into the prepared pan and bake for 22 to 26 minutes, until firm and just beginning to darken slightly.

BEYOND BASIC

In which we broaden our cornbread horizons and cast a wider cornbread net and throw caution to the cornbread wind and any number of other cornbread clichés.

Herein are found such breakfast wonders as Cornmeal Waffles and Griddlecakes, dwelling alongside the sublime and steamy Velvet Spoonbread. Popovers? Sure, we've got those. Hush Puppies to hurl to the dogs? Yep. And biscuits made with peanut butter? Those are my favorite.

Gold Nugget Popovers

Cornmeal shines in simple circumstances. These popovers, an easy variation of a classic recipe, are as simple as it gets. The billowy, crusty popovers accompany meat dishes and hearty stews that other cornbreads might fear to consort with. But they can handle simple pleasures as well: try them warm from the oven with homemade applesauce. And they're embarrassingly easy to make. You can bake popovers in muffin pans, custard cups, or specially designed popover pans. The recipe can be easily doubled or tripled.

2/3 **cup unbleached all-purpose flour**
1/3 **cup cornmeal**
1/2 **teaspoon salt**
1 **cup milk**
2 **large eggs**

1. Preheat your oven to 425°F. Grease your pans or custard cups with vegetable shortening.

2. Combine the flour, cornmeal, and salt in a bowl. Add the milk and eggs and whisk until smooth. Fill each muffin cup, custard cup, or popover cup one-half to two-thirds full.

3. Bake 22 to 28 minutes, until nicely browned. Serve hot.

Carrotbread

This no-flour wonder uses the chiffon technique to achieve loft. The cakelike texture matches the delicate sweetness of the carrot and maple syrup, and there's no need to top it with anything. It's best eaten fresh—but it's so good it's rare to have leftovers, even, I admit, when I'm eating by myself. Heck, with the eggs and carrot, it's almost a meal in itself, but it's also a great soup companion. I adapted this recipe from one of the same name I found in an old cookbook published by El Molino Mills.

1 cup cornmeal

1 cup finely grated carrot (about 1 large carrot)

2 tablespoons canola oil

1 tablespoon maple syrup

1 teaspoon salt

2 large eggs, separated

1.   Preheat your oven to 400°F. Grease a 9 × 9-inch baking pan with vegetable shortening or nonstick cooking spray.

2.   Combine cornmeal, carrot, oil, syrup, and salt in a bowl. Stir in ¾ cup boiling water and set the mixture aside to cool.

3.   Beat the egg yolks with 1 tablespoon cool water and stir them into the cornmeal mixture. In another bowl, beat the egg whites to stiff peaks and fold them gently into the cornmeal mixture until just combined.

4.   Pour the batter into the prepared pan and bake for 20 to 25 minutes, until firm.

Griddlecakes

That's pancakes, pardner. Full o' wee bitty holes, the better to soak up yer syrup.

²⁄₃ cup cornmeal

¹⁄₃ cup unbleached all-purpose flour

1 tablespoon sugar

1 teaspoon baking powder

¹⁄₂ teaspoon salt

1 cup milk

1 large egg, slightly beaten

3 tablespoons unsalted butter, melted, slightly cooled

1. Heat your griddle.

2. Sift the dry ingredients into a bowl, add the milk, egg, and butter, and stir it all until everything is just combined. Pour onto a hot griddle. Flip. Eat.

Cornmeal Waffles

serves 3 or 4

If waffles were used as currency, I suspect that just one of these cornmeal waffles would be worth seven or eight normal waffles. That's how good the toasty cornmeal-wheat germ combination is. I take full credit. You can thank me later. First, eat. You can double the recipe: the waffles freeze well and can be reheated in your toaster.

2 tablespoons toasted wheat germ
1⅓ cups unbleached all-purpose flour
⅔ cup cornmeal
¼ cup sugar
2 teaspoons baking powder
1 teaspoon baking soda
½ teaspoon salt
2¼ cups buttermilk
8 tablespoons (1 stick) unsalted butter, melted, slightly cooled
2 large eggs

1. Preheat your waffle iron.

2. Put the wheat germ into a large bowl, then sift the remaining dry ingredients on top of it. Stir the mixture to distribute the wheat germ. Add the buttermilk, butter, and eggs. Whisk until combined, but don't overmix—there should be many BB-size lumps left in the batter.

3. Pour the batter onto the hot waffle iron. The waffles will turn toasty-brown when they're done. Top them as desired.

Beyond Basic
51

Velvet Spoonbread

serves 6 to 8

One part mush, one part soufflé, and one part cornbread, spoonbread has no equal. Long a staple in southern cuisine, spoonbread has largely failed to find a broader audience. But it deserves more. It accompanies a wide variety of dishes with ease, and often is the main course itself. You're just as likely to encounter it at breakfast as at dinner. Put butter on it and drizzle it with maple syrup or honey. Eat it with applesauce and eggs. Or serve it with ham and redeye gravy.

> 1 cup cornmeal
> 2 tablespoons unsalted butter
> 3 large eggs, separated
> 1 teaspoon sugar
> ¾ teaspoon salt
> 1 cup milk

1.   Preheat your oven to 375°F. Grease a 2-quart baking dish with vegetable shortening or nonstick cooking spray.

2.   Pour 1½ cups boiling water over the cornmeal in a large bowl and whisk until smooth. Add the butter and let it melt while you separate the eggs. Whisk the egg yolks, sugar, and salt into the cornmeal mixture. Gradually whisk in the milk. Allow the mixture to sit 20 minutes while the cornmeal absorbs the milk.

3.   Separately beat the egg whites until they form very stiff peaks, then gradually fold the cornmeal mixture into the egg whites until everything is combined.

4. Pour the batter into the prepared baking dish. Put it in the oven and immediately lower the oven temperature to 350°F. Bake for 65 to 75 minutes, until set.

Owendaw Spoonbread: Stir 1 cup of drained, canned hominy into the batter along with the milk.

Hush Puppies

makes 16 to 18 hush puppies

Whichever story you believe—that hush puppies were originally the scraps from fish fries that were thrown to the hungry
dogs clamoring for food, or that they were bribes offered to
quiet the hounds of Confederate army camps when Union
scouts were near—the fact is that they shut up dogs real quick.
And people, too, who like to eat them alongside fried fish and
coleslaw.

> Oil or shortening for frying
> 1¼ cups cornmeal
> ¾ cup unbleached all-purpose flour
> 1 teaspoon baking powder
> ¾ teaspoon salt
> ¼ teaspoon sugar
> 1 large egg, beaten
> 1 cup milk
> ¼ cup finely minced onion

1. Heat the frying oil in a deep-fryer or heavy skillet, at least
an inch deep, to 370°F.

2. Sift together all the dry ingredients. Stir in the egg, milk,
and onion until everything is well combined.

3. Spoon the wet batter into the hot oil in dollops about the
diameter of a quarter or larger. Fry them until they're evenly
browned, about 3 minutes, turning once. Keep the oil as close
to 370° as possible. Drain the hush puppies on paper towels.
Serve hot.

Tamale Pie

A one-dish classic. I like the punch of the jalapeño peppers. The Drop Biscuit topping bakes up perfectly.

1 pound ground beef
1 medium onion, diced
1 garlic clove, minced
2 jalapeño peppers, seeded and diced
One 14.5-ounce can diced tomatoes and their liquid
One 2.25-ounce can sliced olives, drained
1 tablespoon chili powder
1 teaspoon ground cumin
A few cranks freshly ground black pepper
The makings for Drop Biscuits (page 44)
4 ounces Monterey Jack cheese, shredded

1.   Preheat your oven to 375°F. In a large skillet, cook the beef over medium-high heat until nicely browned, 7 to 9 minutes. Lower the heat to medium-low and add the onion, garlic, and peppers; cook them until tender, about 10 minutes. Add the tomatoes and liquid, olives, chili powder, cumin, and black pepper. Stir everything together and let the mixture cook while you prepare the batter for Drop Biscuits.

2.   When the batter is ready, pour the beef mixture into a 2-quart baking dish, spread the shredded cheese over it, and plop the Drop Biscuit batter on top in about five big plops. Bake for 25 to 35 minutes, until the biscuit topping is crusty and just slightly brown. Serve hot.

Uppity Cornmeal Crepes

makes 12 to 14 crepes, each about 6½ inches.

On occasion, cornmeal surprises even me. Like the time some cornmeal went to the store and bought me some orange juice and bananas when I was too sick to get out of bed. Or the time some cornmeal picked my mom up from the airport (although it went to the wrong concourse). Or these recipes, where cornmeal performs with aplomb in dinner crepes. True, the dessert crepes benefit from the smoother texture that corn flour provides. The technique of cooking the perfect crepe is tricky, but you'll get the hang of it. It only took me nine years. As for the fillings/toppings for these crepes, you're on your own. What do you think this is, a crepe book?

DINNER CREPES

½ cup cornmeal

½ cup unbleached all-purpose flour

1 cup milk

¼ cup water

2 large eggs

3 tablespoons unsalted butter, melted, slightly cooled

¼ teaspoon salt

1. Lightly grease the bottom of a crepe pan or heavy, flat-bottomed 8-inch skillet (I prefer a well-seasoned cast iron skillet) with a very thin layer of oil or butter and then wipe it out with a paper towel, leaving only a thin film of grease. Let the skillet heat up over medium heat (or slightly higher).

2. Whisk all the ingredients together until the batter is smooth. Pour about 3 tablespoons of batter (for an 8-inch skillet) into the hot skillet, tilting the skillet to quickly distribute the batter over its entire bottom. The crepe will cook quickly, with little beads of water rising to its surface. If it burns immediately, the skillet is too hot.

3. Loosen the sides of each crepe as it cooks with a knife and peek under the crepe to see how brown it is. When it's very light brown, slide a thin spatula or flexible knife beneath the crepe a few times to dislodge it, then invert the skillet over a paper towel. The crepe should fall right out, where it can cool for a few minutes. Make sure to stir the batter each time before pouring a new crepe—otherwise all the cornmeal will sink to the bottom of the bowl.

DESSERT CREPES

²⁄₃ **cup unbleached all-purpose flour**

¹⁄₃ **cup corn flour**

1 cup milk

¹⁄₄ **cup water**

2 large eggs

3 tablespoons unsalted butter, melted, slightly cooled

2 tablespoons sugar

¹⁄₈ **teaspoon salt**

Same technique as dinner crepes.

Nut-Butter Biscuits

Using peanut butter as the shortening in these biscuits accentuates the toasted flavor of the cornmeal, making for a satisfying biscuit that tastes great by itself but accepts toppings with ease. A smooth or creamy commercial peanut butter works best, not a natural or chunky peanut butter. Buttermilk can be substituted for the cream, but the resulting biscuits won't be as exceptional. If you have trouble handling the wet batter, just cut the biscuits without folding the batter, or drop big spoonfuls of the batter right onto the baking sheet.

1½ cups unbleached all-purpose flour
⅔ cup cornmeal
1 tablespoon baking powder
¼ teaspoon baking soda
½ teaspoon salt
6 tablespoons peanut butter
1 cup buttermilk
½ cup heavy cream

1. Preheat your oven to 450°F.

2. Sift the dry ingredients into a medium bowl. Cut in the peanut butter with a pastry cutter until the mixture resembles a coarse meal. Add the buttermilk and cream and stir vigorously until everything is combined and smooth.

3. Turn the dough out onto a well-floured work surface, pat it out into a thick, rough rectangle, fold the rectangle in half

and press it gently together, then pat it into a rectangle again. Repeat this patting/folding process a total of three or four times. Don't be afraid to dust the dough with a little flour in order to handle it.

4. Finally, pat or roll the dough out to about ¾ inch thick. Cut it with a sharp biscuit cutter. Place the biscuits on an ungreased cookie sheet and bake them for 10 to 16 minutes, until they're light brown.

On the matter of nubbins (a.k.a. "bits and pieces"): When you cut biscuits with a round biscuit cutter, you're typically left with many little odd-shaped nubbins. Of course, you can always gather these nubbins, press them together, and cut more biscuits from them. But those cobbled biscuits won't be as pretty or tender as the original biscuits. One solution is to cut square biscuits by slicing the dough with a sharp pizza cutter, leaving significantly fewer nubbins. But I like round biscuits, so I just always bake the nubbins as is, crumble them into a cereal bowl, put berries, honey, and milk over them, and consume.

Corn Fritters

Serve these rich fritters alongside meat dishes or eat them for dessert. Some people drizzle syrup over them, but I like to roll mine in sugar.

> **Oil or shortening for frying**
> **1 cup unbleached all-purpose flour**
> **1 teaspoon baking powder**
> **¾ teaspoon salt**
> **2 large eggs**
> **½ cup milk**
> **2 teaspoons canola oil**
> **¾ cup corn kernels, canned (drained) or**
> **frozen (thawed)**
> **Sugar for coating, optional**

1.   Either fire up your deep-fryer or heat at least 2 inches of shortening or oil over medium heat in a heavy pan. Heat the oil to 375°F.

2.   Sift the flour, baking powder, and salt into a bowl. Separately beat together the eggs, milk, and canola oil. Add the corn kernels to this wet mixture and then pour it all into the dry mixture and stir until everything is combined.

3.   Drop spoonfuls of the batter into the hot oil and fry until each fritter is golden brown on each side, 2 to 3 minutes total, turning as necessary. Remove the fritters to drain on paper towels. If you want to coat them in sugar, do it while they are still warm by rolling the fritters in a bowl of sugar.

Boston Brown Bread

This molasses-flavored steamed bread is an American classic, traditionally served with baked beans. The bread also toasts nicely.

1 cup rye flour
1 cup cornmeal
1 cup whole wheat flour
1½ teaspoons baking soda
¾ teaspoon salt
2 cups buttermilk
¾ cup molasses

1. Sift the dry ingredients into a large mixing bowl. Stir in the buttermilk and molasses. Beat the mixture for 2 minutes.

2. Divide the batter among 3 vegetable shortening greased, clean, 20-ounce cans. Improvise a steamer by setting the cans in a large stockpot on a rack that is somehow raised off the bottom of the pot—by putting a few custard cups or ramekins under it, for instance. Cover the cans with foil, then place them on the rack. Add water to the pot, just enough so that it doesn't touch the rack. Cover the pot, bring the water to a simmer, and steam the bread for 2½ to 3 hours, adding water as necessary. The bread will form nice little domes on top as it bakes, and will firm up as it gets close to finished. You may be able to open the bottoms of the cans with a can opener so you can get the bread out.

SWEET CORNBREADS

In which **sugar** in its many guises
makes a triumphant and celebratory
appearance at the **height** of the **third**
act of our **cornmeal** saga.

Do you like caramel corn? Then try Caramel Corncake. And is there anything quite as good as a blackberry cobbler topped with crusty cornmeal cobbles? No. Also, see how cornmeal breathes new life into sugar cookies. And don't miss the fruit-friendly Summer Kitchen Pound Cake and its comely cousin, Lemon-Cornmeal Everyday Cake.

Crinkle-Top Sugar Cookies

makes about 36 cookies

I generally don't care for sugar cookies. My sweet tooth doesn't usually consider something dessert unless it's buried under chocolate, topped with streusel, filled with pastry cream, or flammable. But the toasted flavor of the cornmeal rescues these cookies from blandness and also lends them extra crispness. They keep for at least a couple of weeks in an airtight container, and if you use cultured butter they develop a friendly sourness as the days pass.

> 8 tablespoons (1 stick) unsalted butter (or unsalted cultured butter), softened
> 1 cup sugar
> 1 large egg
> 1 teaspoon pure vanilla extract
> 1 cup unbleached all-purpose flour
> ½ cup cornmeal
> 1 teaspoon baking powder
> ½ teaspoon salt
> Sugar for the glazed tops

1.   Preheat your oven to 350°F. Get out 2 cookie sheets.

2.   Cream the butter and sugar in a medium bowl. (I like to use the butter wrapper to lightly grease my cookie sheets at this point.) Whisk in the egg and vanilla until smooth. Separately sift the flour, cornmeal, baking powder, and salt. Gradually stir into the batter, just until smooth.

3. Here's the cosmetic part to ensure a beautiful cookie: make a ball with about 2 teaspoons of dough by rolling it gently between your palms. Place the balls about 3½ inches apart on a cookie sheet. Take something with a nice flat bottom, preferably see-through—like a glass—dip it in cool water, dip it into a bowl of sugar, then use it to flatten a dough ball. The result should be a thin, uniformly round disc about 2 inches across with a crust of damp sugar pressed into it. Repeat this process, re-wetting and sugaring the bottom of the glass between each cookie. The cookies will spread only a tiny bit as they bake.

4. Bake the cookies, one sheet at a time, for 8 to 12 minutes, until set and just *barely* starting to brown around the edges. Allow the cookies to cool for a few minutes on the cookie sheet before removing them to cool on a rack.

Orange Sugar Cookies: In place of the vanilla, add 1 teaspoon orange juice and 2 teaspoons grated orange zest (dried by pressing it between 2 paper towels).

Lemon Sugar Cookies: Same thing—1 teaspoon lemon juice, 2 teaspoons grated, dried lemon zest.

(Try dividing your dough in half and making lemon and orange sugar cookies in one batch. Don't forget to halve the quantities of zest and juice.)

Curly Churros
(Mexican Fritters)

I call them grease sticks. But they're real good.

Oil or shortening for frying
4 tablespoons (½ stick) unsalted butter
1 tablespoon sugar
½ teaspoon salt
½ cup unbleached all-purpose flour
½ cup cornmeal
Cinnamon sugar, made with 1 cup sugar and
    2 teaspoons ground cinnamon, optional
2 large eggs
Confectioners' sugar, optional

1. Get your frying oil heated to 375°F. It should be at least 2 inches deep, preferably more.

2. In a medium saucepan, bring 1 cup water, the butter, sugar, and salt to a moderate boil, stirring regularly. Reduce the heat to low. Add the flour and cornmeal all at once and stir until the dough comes together in a ball, pulling away from the pan. Let the dough cool a couple of minutes (make the cinnamon sugar now in a shallow pan if you wish). Add the eggs and whisk them into the dough until smooth.

3. Spoon the dough into a pastry bag or a cookie press fitted with a medium star tip about ½ inch wide. When the oil is ready, pipe 5-inch strips of the dough into the oil. The chur-

ros will curl up on their own. Fry the churros until they're lightly browned on one side, then turn them and brown them on the other side. The frying time will depend on how big your churros are, but it will be approximately 90 seconds on each side. Keep your oil temperature as constant as possible.

4. Drain the churros on paper towels, then dredge them through the cinnamon sugar while they're still hot. Or dust them with confectioners' sugar. Eat them while they're warm.

Apple Skillet Flipcake

Think of this as a hillbilly tart. In the spirit of old-timey corn-meal cookery, this homey cake is baked in a cast iron skillet, which cooks the cake evenly and ensures a nice brown bottom (which later becomes the top). Also in the Ozarky spirit of this cake, instead of calling it an upside-down cake, which is exactly what it is, I call it a flipcake, which is a much better name anyway. Note: if your skillet is much less than 2 inches deep, I recommend using a 9-inch skillet to avoid overflowing.

3 tablespoons unsalted butter, melted, plus
    2 tablespoons, softened
3 tablespoons brown sugar
⅓ cup chopped English or black walnuts
1⅓ cups diced apple (about 1 large apple or
    1½ small apples)
Ground cinnamon for dusting
½ cup unbleached all-purpose flour
½ cup cornmeal
⅓ cup sugar
1 teaspoon baking powder
¼ teaspoon salt
½ cup milk
1 large egg
½ teaspoon pure vanilla extract

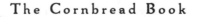

1.   Preheat your oven to 375°F.

2.   For the topping, pour the 3 tablespoons melted butter into an 8-inch cast iron skillet and sprinkle the brown sugar and walnuts over it. Microwave the apples for 90 seconds and pour off any water. Layer the apples over the walnuts and dust them generously with cinnamon.

3.   For the cake batter, sift the flour, cornmeal, sugar, baking powder, and salt into a medium bowl. Add the milk and the 2 tablespoons softened butter and stir for 1 minute. Then add the egg and vanilla and stir for another minute. Pour the batter into the skillet and spread it evenly over the apples.

4.   Bake the cake for 24 to 30 minutes, until lightly browned at the edges and firm to the touch. After removing the cake from the oven, slide a knife around the cake's rim to loosen it in the pan, then invert it onto a serving plate.

Black Mountain Sorghum Cake

makes 9 pieces

In the shadow of Black Mountain, in the Missouri Ozarks, my great-grandparents made their own sorghum molasses every autumn. They cut the sorghum cane, stripped it of its leaves, then fed it through their mule-powered mill to extract the cane juice. This juice was boiled down to make sorghum. One of their favorite uses for sorghum was a rich gingerbread-like cake. Most of the family didn't like ginger, so they left it out, but you could add a teaspoon to this recipe to make it a true gingerbread. You can also substitute molasses for sorghum, though that's somewhat like substituting corn syrup for maple syrup. Dust the finished cake with confectioners' sugar and serve it with whipped cream, applesauce, or a scoop of cinnamon ice cream.

8 tablespoons (1 stick) unsalted butter, softened
¼ cup sugar
1 large egg
¾ cup sorghum or molasses (not blackstrap)
1¼ cups unbleached all-purpose flour
¾ cup corn flour
1 teaspoon baking soda
1 teaspoon ground cinnamon
½ teaspoon salt
¼ teaspoon ground cloves
Confectioners' sugar, optional

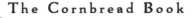

1. Preheat your oven to 350°F. Grease (with butter or vegetable shortening) and flour a 9 × 9-inch baking pan.

2. Cream the butter and sugar in a medium bowl. Beat in the egg, then the sorghum, and then 1 cup of water. The mixture will look clotted.

3. Sift the flours, baking soda, cinnamon, salt, and cloves, add them to the wet ingredients, and whisk until smooth. Pour the batter into the pan and bake for 30 to 40 minutes, until well set in the middle. If desired, dust with confectioners' sugar.

Berry Patch Cobbler

serves 6

Wild blackberries hate people: they grow thorns to repel us, and they've been remarkably successful, all over their territory, in recruiting legions upon legions of mosquitoes, ticks, and chiggers to guard them. Upon legions. Not to mention poison ivy and the occasional rattlesnake and/or copperhead. Whenever I pick wild blackberries, I seem to receive one chigger bite for each berry I pick. This is a hefty price to pay, but when the cobbler comes out of the oven, it all becomes worthwhile. If you don't have wild blackberries, frozen blackberries are almost as good, and you don't even have to thaw them.

½ cup sugar

4½ teaspoons cornstarch

1 teaspoon ground cinnamon

Pinch of salt

1 tablespoon freshly squeezed orange juice

½ cup unbleached all-purpose flour

½ cup cornmeal

3 tablespoons sugar

¼ teaspoon plus ⅛ teaspoon salt

¼ teaspoon baking powder

¼ teaspoon baking soda

3 tablespoons unsalted butter, softened

½ cup buttermilk

4 to 5 cups fresh or frozen blackberries
    (5 cups if berries are "jumbo")

Ground cinnamon for sprinkling, optional

1. Preheat your oven to 400°F.

2. In a nonreactive medium saucepan, combine the sugar, cornstarch, cinnamon, and salt. Slowly add ½ cup water and the orange juice, stirring constantly. Heat the mixture over medium-high heat, stirring, until it is bubbly and thick. Remove the pan from the heat and set it aside.

3. Sift the flour, cornmeal, sugar, salt, baking powder, and baking soda into a large bowl. With a pastry cutter, cut in the butter until the mixture resembles coarse meal. Add the buttermilk and stir until just combined.

4. Place the berries in a 2-quart baking dish. Pour the warm syrup mixture over them, then stir to coat and distribute the syrup. Drop the crust mixture onto the berries in four to six big "cobbles." Dust the crust with cinnamon if you wish. Bake for 24 to 30 minutes, until the crust is slightly brown. Cobbler is best served when it has cooled for an hour or two. Serve with vanilla or cinnamon ice cream.

Blueberry Cobbler: Blueberries are much easier to find fresh, even midwinter. Substitute blueberries for the blackberries, and 1½ teaspoons lime juice for the orange juice.

Zaletti

These diamond-shaped Venetian cookies are lemony and crumbly and just sweet enough. And the dry cookie contrasts perfectly with the soft raisins. The softer and fresher your raisins, the better. Just beware of overbaking these cookies—you really only want the bottoms to be pale brown.

1 cup cornmeal
1 cup unbleached all-purpose flour
⅓ cup sugar
1 teaspoon baking powder
¼ teaspoon salt
8 tablespoons (1 stick) unsalted butter, softened
¾ cup raisins
1 large egg
1 large egg yolk
1 teaspoon pure vanilla extract
Zest of 1 lemon

1.   Preheat your oven to 350°F. Line 2 baking sheets with parchment paper.

2.   Sift the cornmeal, flour, sugar, baking powder, and salt into a large mixing bowl. Stir until well combined. Cut in the butter with a pastry cutter until the mixture is crumbly and resembles coarse meal. Stir in the raisins.

3.   Separately whisk together the egg, egg yolk, vanilla, and lemon zest. Stir into the cornmeal/butter mixture until the

mixture is uniform. The dough will be stiff, and you may have to use your hands. Finally, knead the dough a few times in the bowl until it forms a cohesive mass.

4. Divide the dough in half. On a lightly floured work surface, roll each half out into a rope, 20 inches long. Flatten the rope gently with the palm of your hand, just so it's about ½ inch thick, or slightly bigger. Cut the flattened rope on a diagonal so that the cookies are diamond-shaped. Each rope will make about 12 cookies.

5. Transfer the cookies to the baking sheets and bake one sheet at a time for 12 to 16 minutes, until the zaletti are firm and lightly browned on the bottoms. Let the cookies cool on a rack.

Persimmon Coffee Cake

Persimmons are one of the only wild fruits that grows in the part of Missouri where I grew up. If you've never tasted them before, this coffee cake is a good introduction. The persimmons you find in the store are not likely to have come from the Midwest, but they'll work. If you live in an area where persimmons grow, look for them at your local farmer's market in the autumn.

> ¾ cup persimmon pulp (milled from about 1 pint
> native persimmons or 2 large supermarket
> persimmons)
> 1½ cups unbleached all-purpose flour
> ½ cup cornmeal
> 1 cup sugar
> 1 tablespoon baking powder
> 1 teaspoon salt
> ½ teaspoon ground cinnamon
> ¾ cup milk
> 4 tablespoons (½ stick) unsalted butter, softened
> 2 large eggs, slightly beaten
>
> TOPPING
> ½ cup packed brown sugar
> ½ cup chopped nuts
> 2 tablespoons unsalted butter, melted
> 4 teaspoons flour
> 2 teaspoons ground cinnamon

1. Preheat your oven to 350°F and grease a 9 × 9-inch baking pan with butter or vegetable shortening. Make your persimmon pulp by running your persimmons through a food mill or mashing them through a strainer.

2. Sift the flour, cornmeal, sugar, baking powder, salt, and cinnamon into a mixing bowl. Stir the mixture briefly. Then stir in the milk, butter, eggs, and persimmon pulp, until well combined. Pour the batter into the prepared pan.

3. Put all the topping ingredients in a small bowl and stir them until combined. Crumble this topping over the coffee cake. Bake for 42 to 48 minutes, until well set and a knife inserted in the middle comes out clean.

Raspberry Coffee Cake: Persimmons can be difficult to find, but raspberries are pretty easy to come by, even if you pay a dollar per berry. Of course, fresh local berries are best. The cake made with raspberries is a nice dusky rose color and has a soft floral aroma. Substitute ¾ cup mashed fresh red raspberries for the persimmon pulp. It takes about 1¾ cups of fresh berries to make ¾ cup mashed pulp.

Choco-Corno-Espresso-Almondo Biscotti

makes about 30 biscotti

In my coffeehouse days I lost three molars and one bicuspid to biscotti that were stone hard. The cornmeal in these biscotti lends them a controlled crumbliness that prevents dental trauma. And the toasted flavor of twice-baked cornmeal is lovely and pairs well with semisweet chocolate. Putting cornmeal in biscotti is not a novel idea—the Italians have done it for a long time. These keep for a couple of weeks at room temperature in an airtight container.

1⅓ cups unbleached all-purpose flour
⅔ cup cornmeal
1 teaspoon baking powder
½ teaspoon salt
½ cup turbinado sugar
¼ cup almond paste, cut into small pieces
3 tablespoons unsalted butter, cold, cut into cubes
2 large eggs
1 teaspoon vanilla extract

CHOCOLATE TOPPING
½ cup semisweet chocolate chips
2 teaspoons instant espresso powder, optional
2 teaspoons vegetable shortening
Turbinado sugar for sprinkling, optional

1. Preheat your oven to 350°F. Lightly grease a baking sheet with butter or vegetable shortening.

2. Sift the flour, cornmeal, baking powder, and salt into a mixing bowl. Stir in the sugar. Cut in the almond paste and butter with a pastry cutter until the largest lumps remaining are about pea-size. Stir in the eggs and vanilla.

3. At this point the dough will have wet clumps, but it will be far from mixed. Stir vigorously for a bit, then mix the dough with your hands. The goal is a stiff dough that has just incorporated all the dry ingredients and will stick together when pressed. To this end, you will likely need to add 1 to 4 teaspoons of water to the dough. Don't worry about visible lumps of butter or almond paste.

4. As soon as the dough holds together and is well mixed, divide it in half. Shape each half into a thick rope and press each rope onto a lightly greased (or parchment paper–lined) cookie sheet. Flatten each rope into an approximately 12 × 3-inch rectangle. Bake the rectangles for 16 to 20 minutes, until well set and just beginning to brown a bit on the edges.

5. Remove the rectangles from the oven and let them cool for a few minutes, then slice them into individual biscotti between ½ and ¾ inch thick. Place the biscotti on their sides on the cookie sheet and return to the oven for 8 minutes. At that point, flip the biscotti onto their other sides and bake another 8 to 12 minutes, until they look toasty but not over-browned on the edges. Remove the biscotti and allow them to cool. They will still be slightly moist and flexible at this point, but they will dry as they cool.

6. While the biscotti cool, melt the chocolate, espresso powder (if desired), and vegetable shortening in a double boiler over very low heat until smooth. Dip the sides of the cooled biscotti into the chocolate and shake off the excess. Sprinkle the chocolate coatings generously with turbinado sugar, if desired. Refrigerate the biscotti until the chocolate sets.

Caramel Corncake

I wish I could take credit for this recipe, but it is wholly my mother's invention. It's a homey dessert, the kind I love. It's also a remarkable lesson in the chemistry of cooking. How, after all, does the crusty and tender cake end up floating upon a golden sea of caramel sauce?

¾ cup unbleached all-purpose flour
¼ cup cornmeal
1¼ cups packed brown sugar
2 teaspoons baking powder
¾ teaspoon salt
2 tablespoons toasted wheat germ
½ cup milk
2 tablespoons unsalted butter, melted
1½ teaspoons pure vanilla extract

1. Preheat your oven to 325°F and grease a 2-quart baking dish with butter or vegetable shortening.

2. Sift the flour, cornmeal, ½ cup of the brown sugar, baking powder, and salt into a mixing bowl. Stir in the wheat germ. Stir in the milk, melted butter, and vanilla until the batter is well combined.

3. Spread the batter into the prepared dish and sprinkle the remaining ¾ cup of brown sugar over it. Now for the interesting part: pour 1½ cups of very hot water over the cake. Bake for 45 to 50 minutes, until very lightly browned. Serve warm with ice cream.

Sweet Potato Cupcakes

It's like holding the power of a pumpkin pie in the palm of your hand! *Pow! Bam! Kerplooonk! Blat!* Or any other comic book noise you can think of! And here's the beauty part! Get ready for this! You don't put frosting on them! No! No! YOU TOP THEM WITH FRESH WHIPPED CREAM! *Schmack! Ploink! Braak! You win!*

¾ cup sugar

⅓ cup (5⅓ tablespoons) unsalted butter, softened

1 large egg

½ cup cooked and mashed sweet potato
   (or canned pumpkin, which makes a cupcake
   with lovely texture and loft)

1 cup unbleached all-purpose flour

½ cup corn flour

1 teaspoon baking powder

½ teaspoon salt

½ teaspoon ground cinnamon

¼ teaspoon ground allspice

¼ teaspoon grated nutmeg

¾ cup milk

1 cup heavy cream for whipping, optional

1. Preheat your oven to 400°F. Line a muffin pan with 12 cupcake cups.

2. Cream the sugar and butter in a large mixing bowl. Beat in the egg and sweet potato. Separately sift the flour, baking powder, salt, and spices. Add about half the dry mixture to the sweet potato mixture and stir until incorporated. Add half the milk to the sweet potato mixture and stir. Then stir in the remaining dry mixture. And finally stir in the remaining milk. You should have a nice, smooth cake batter.

3. Distribute the batter evenly among the cupcake cups, and bake for 17 to 22 minutes, until well set and a clean knife inserted into the middle of a cupcake comes out clean. Cool and top with . . . FRESH WHIPPED CREAM! *Bonk! Splat! Boing! You win!*

Sour Cream Pie Crust

a generous crust recipe, enough for a 9- or 10-inch pie

The sour cream flavor here is a suitable partner for any sweet pie filling, but it also pairs well with savory flavors. It's also a remarkably forgiving crust—easy to make, easy to roll out, easy to handle. And it browns beautifully. This is the one-crust recipe here, easily doubled.

¾ cup unbleached all-purpose flour
½ cup corn flour
½ teaspoon salt
¼ cup plus 2 tablespoons vegetable shortening
½ cup (4 ounces) sour cream

1. Sift the flour, corn flour, and salt into a mixing bowl. Cut in the shortening with a pastry cutter until the largest remaining lumps of shortening are pea-size. Add the sour cream and stir just until the dough begins to come together and the sour cream is sufficiently distributed. If the dough is too stiff for you to stir, mix it with your hands and fingers.

2. Make the dough into a ball, wrap in plastic wrap, and chill it for 30 minutes. Roll the crust out to the desired size on a well-floured work surface or sheet of waxed paper.

3. Bake as directed in whatever pie recipe you're using, or prick the shell liberally with the tines of a fork and bake it empty in a 425°F oven for 8 to 10 minutes, until lightly browned.

Biscuits au Mais

My take on this Basque cookie ends up being a kind of short-bread, really. If you put any more butter into these things, they'd turn into cows. Believe me, I've seen it happen.

1 cup (2 sticks) unsalted butter, softened
⅔ cup sugar
1 cup cornmeal
1 large egg
1 teaspoon salt
1¼ cups unbleached all-purpose flour

1. Preheat your oven to 300°F. Set out 2 baking sheets. Don't grease them.

2. Cream the butter and sugar in a medium bowl. Add the cornmeal, egg, and salt and stir until smooth. Then slowly stir in the flour, adding it just until the mixture comes together in a cohesive mass. It may or may not take the full amount of flour.

3. Take the dough in your palms and form it into a ball, then dust it with flour. On a floured work surface, gently pat or roll the dough until it is about ¼ inch or so thick. With a pizza cutter, slice the dough into 2-inch squares and place the squares on the baking sheets, leaving at least 1 inch between the squares.

4. Bake for 35 to 45 minutes, until the cookies are dry and very lightly browned on the edges. Let the cookies cool on the baking sheet before moving them to an airtight container.

Summer Kitchen Pound Cake

serves 8

One bleary-eyed morning I mistook a loaf of this pound cake for a loaf of white bread, and I proceeded to make jam-on-toast with it. It was the best jam-on-toast I've ever had. When I'm not eating it for breakfast, my favorite way to eat my favorite cake is with sliced and sugared strawberries. The yogurt in the batter improves the cake's texture, but an almost equally great cake can be made with—drumroll here—water.

1 cup (2 sticks) unsalted butter, softened
1½ cups sugar
3 large eggs
½ cup plain yogurt (or any flavor) (or water)
   (milk would work, too) (or sour cream)
1 teaspoon pure vanilla extract
1½ cups unbleached all-purpose flour
½ cup corn flour
1½ teaspoons baking powder
¼ teaspoon salt
Poppyseeds for sprinkling, optional

1.   Preheat your oven to 325°F. Butter and flour a 9 × 5-inch loaf pan.

2.   Cream the butter and sugar in a large bowl. Beat in the eggs individually. In a separate bowl, combine the yogurt and vanilla. In another bowl, sift the flour, corn flour, baking powder, and salt.

3. Add about a quarter of the yogurt mixture to the butter-egg mixture and stir until incorporated. Then add about a quarter of the flour mixture to the butter-egg mixture and stir it in. Repeat these steps until all the ingredients are combined and the batter is smooth. Pour the batter into the prepared loaf pan. Sprinkle the loaf with poppyseeds, if desired.

4. Bake for 60 to 80 minutes, until a knife inserted in the middle comes out clean. Watch the cake carefully near the end of its baking, lest its sides and bottom burn. Let the cake cool in the pan before serving.

Lemon-Cornmeal Everyday Cake: This sunshine-yellow, less-rich cousin of Summer Kitchen Pound Cake is the perfect companion for fresh fruit. You can ice it with a thin glaze, but it's perfect when unadorned. Follow the directions for Summer Kitchen Pound Cake, but use only 1 stick of butter. Substitute cornmeal for the corn flour, and in place of the vanilla use the juice and zest of 1 lemon. Bake the cake in a 9 × 9-inch pan lined with parchment paper on the bottom and buttered on the sides. Bake the cake for 45 to 55 minutes, until golden and firm.

Indian Pudding

Attention: this is not a bread. So sue me. Indian pudding is a cornmeal-based molasses-flavored custard that is absolutely fantastic when served warm with a scoop of vanilla ice cream. It's remarkably good cold, too. It's a great classic American cornmeal dish that is underappreciated and that's why I'm including it here. Not as if I have to explain myself to the likes of you.

3¼ cups milk
⅓ cup cornmeal
½ cup molasses (not blackstrap)
¾ teaspoon salt
1 tablespoon unsalted butter
1 large egg
¼ cup sugar
½ teaspoon ground cinnamon
½ teaspoon ground ginger
⅓ cup raisins, optional

1. Preheat your oven to 325°F. In a medium saucepan, heat the milk, cornmeal, molasses, and salt over medium-high heat, stirring constantly, until the mixture is thickened, about 10 minutes. Remove the pan from the heat and add the butter to it, stirring until the butter is melted.

2. Separately combine the egg, sugar, cinnamon, ginger, and raisins (if desired). Slowly stir this mixture into the hot milk/cornmeal mixture. Pour the batter into a 1½- or 2-quart baking dish and bake for 60 to 75 minutes, until softly set and dark.

YEAST CORNBREADS

In which yeast, that frothing fungus,
infuses our cornbreads with a
breath of air, making them billow
and puff and smell so nice.

From the classic Anadama Batter Bread and Cornmeal Pizza Dough to the sweet Honey Snail and the unique New Zuni Bread. And introducing three breads made in part with flour milled from popped popcorn: Popcorn White Loaf, Popcorn Pita Bread, and—perhaps the best of all—Popcorn Focaccia.

Popcorn White Loaf

makes 2 loaves

If I accomplish nothing worthwhile in this lifetime (and that seems to be a possibility), and all my novels go unread, and my lovely little cornbread book goes out of print within moments of hitting the shelves, and everyone laughs at the recipes, I will still be happy if just one person (other than me) makes the following recipe once.

These popcorn loaves, based on a basic white bread recipe, are inviting, versatile, and so darn good. I think the popcorn flour improves not only the flavor but the texture. The bread is perfect while still warm, doused with honey and butter, but it also toasts with grace for breakfast, produces great sandwiches, and makes what is my favorite French toast when it's about a day and a half old.

Freeze slices for later toasting or reheating.

Two ¼-ounce packets or 4½ teaspoons active dry
　　or instant yeast
1 tablespoon sugar
2 teaspoons salt
2 tablespoons unsalted butter, softened
2½ cups popcorn flour
5½ to 7 cups unbleached all-purpose flour

1.　Make your popcorn flour according to the instructions on page 22.

2.　Dissolve the yeast in 1 cup lukewarm water (110°F) in a large bowl. Add all the other ingredients, except that you should add only 3 cups of the all-purpose flour. Add another 1½ cups of lukewarm water and stir the mixture until it is smooth. Slowly stir in the remaining flour until the dough is just stiff enough to be kneadable by hand. The goal is a rather soft dough. Turn the dough onto a floured work surface and knead by hand for 5 to 7 minutes, until it is smooth and elastic, adding only as much flour as needed to prevent the dough from sticking to your hands and work surface. If you see some big popcorn kernels that didn't pop fully and didn't get ground up, you can pull them out if you want.

3. Place the dough in a vegetable shortening greased bowl, cover it with a wet towel, and let it rise in a warm place until doubled in bulk—45 to 60 minutes. Punch the dough down, turn it over, cover it again, and let it rise a second time until almost doubled, 20 to 30 minutes. Divide the dough in half. Butter two 9 × 5-inch loaf pans.

4. Shape each loaf by first patting it out into a rectangle with a width equal to the length of your loaf pan. Fold the top third of the rectangle down onto itself—like folding a letter— and seal it with your fingers. Fold it again and pinch the seam closed. Then fold the loaf's ends in slightly and pinch them shut, too. Now place the loaf in the pan, gently plumping and shaping it so that it is uniform and even.

5. Cover the loaf pans with the damp towel and let the loaves rise a final time until they fill the pans and bulge beautifully, 40 to 60 minutes. Meanwhile, preheat your oven to 375°F. Bake for 35 to 45 minutes, until the loaves are nicely browned and hollow-sounding when tapped on the bottom. Turn the loaves out of the pans and allow them to cool on a wire rack for 15 or 20 minutes before slicing.

Portuguese Cornbread (Broa)

This modest but lovely round loaf is common throughout Portugal, although the ratio of cornmeal to flour varies from region to region. It's traditionally served with kale and sausage soup, but it's good enough to go with anything. A baking stone produces a superior bread.

> One ¼-ounce packet or 2¼ teaspoons active dry
>   or instant yeast
> ½ cup lukewarm milk (110°F)
> 1 cup cornmeal (preferably whole-grain), plus more
>   for dusting
> 1 teaspoon salt
> 1 teaspoon olive oil
> 2 to 2½ cups unbleached all-purpose flour

1.   In a small bowl, let the yeast dissolve in 1 cup lukewarm water (110°F). Meanwhile, stir together the milk, cornmeal, salt, and oil in a large bowl. Add the dissolved yeast mixture and whisk until smooth. (It's okay if there are small clumps.) Slowly add the flour, while stirring, until you have a nice kneadable dough. Turn the dough out onto a floured counter and knead for about 5 minutes, adding only as much flour as necessary to prevent the dough from sticking. Form the dough into a ball, place it in a vegetable shortening greased bowl, cover, and let it rise in a warm place until doubled in bulk, about 1 hour.

2. Punch the dough down, then knead it for another 5 minutes. Shape the dough into a round loaf and put it on a pizza peel dusted liberally and widely with cornmeal (the loaf will grow much broader as it rises). Cover the loaf and let it rise again until doubled, about 45 minutes.

3. Heat your baking stone on the bottom rack of your oven at 425°F for at least 30 minutes. Also heat an empty loaf pan in the oven, below and to the side of the stone. Dust the surface of the risen loaf liberally with cornmeal, then slide it quickly into the oven, onto the stone. Immediately pour 1 cup of water with 2 ice cubes in it into the empty loaf pan and shut the oven door.

4. Bake the bread for 20 to 30 minutes, until the loaf is golden and hollow sounding when tapped on the bottom.

Cornmeal Pizza Dough

makes 2 medium pizzas

If you love thin-crust pizza, it's hard to beat a dough with a little cornmeal in it. Double or triple the recipe if you wish. A baking stone is a must if you want that perfect thin-crust crispiness, but you can turn out a good pizza by baking it in a pan, too. For a thicker, doughier pizza crust, I recommend Popcorn Focaccia (page 112).

> Two ¼-ounce packets or 4½ teaspoons active dry or
>   instant yeast
> 1 cup lukewarm milk (110°F)
> ¼ cup olive oil
> ¼ teaspoon sugar
> 2 cups unbleached all-purpose flour
> ½ cup cornmeal
> 1 teaspoon salt

1. Sprinkle the yeast into the milk and let it dissolve in a large bowl. Stir in the olive oil and sugar. Sift the flour, cornmeal, and salt, then add them to the yeast mixture. Stir the dough vigorously for a minute, then turn the dough onto a floured work surface and knead it until it is smooth and elastic, about 5 minutes, adding only as much flour as needed to keep it from sticking to your hands and the counter.

2. Gather the dough into a ball and put it into a large bowl greased with olive oil. Turn the dough in the bowl so that the oil coats its entire surface, then cover the bowl with plastic wrap and let the dough rise until nearly doubled in size, 30 to

50 minutes. Near the end of the first rise, heat your oven and baking stone (if you're using one) to 450°F. (You want to allow the stone to heat for at least 30 minutes before baking the pizzas.)

3.   Punch the dough down, cover it again, and allow it to rise a second time until doubled or slightly bigger, 15 to 25 minutes. Divide the dough in half, and, on a cornmeal-sprinkled pizza peel, roll each half out to a thin circle, 12 to 15 inches in diameter. Top with your favorite pizza toppings, but avoid overloading the crust. Bake on the baking stone for 8 to 12 minutes, until lightly browned on the edges.

New Zuni Bread

I've modified this versatile Native American yeast bread to be slightly lighter in texture and a bit mellower without sacrificing its heartiness and smoothness. And the soy flour gives it a flavor and softness that are one of a kind. This bread toasts and freezes well, which is one reason I scaled this recipe to make two loaves.

If you're going to dirty every mixing bowl you own, why not get two loaves out of the deal instead of just one?

> One ¼-ounce packet or 2¼ teaspoons active dry
>   or instant yeast
> 2¾ cups whole wheat flour
> ½ cup canola oil
> 6 tablespoons honey
> 1½ teaspoons salt
> 1¾ cups unbleached all-purpose flour
> ½ cup soy flour
> 1 cup cornmeal

1. Combine the yeast, ½ cup of the whole wheat flour, and ½ cup lukewarm (110°F) water. Stir to dissolve the yeast. Separately whisk together the canola oil, honey, and 2 cups of lukewarm water.

2. Sift together the salt, all-purpose flour, and 1½ cups of the whole wheat flour; add to the yeast mixture. Add the oil/honey mixture to the yeast mixture, too. With an electric mixer, beat this thin dough for 8 to 10 minutes.

3. Add the soy flour, the remaining ¾ cup of whole wheat flour, and the cornmeal. Stir until everything is incorporated, then turn the dough out onto a floured surface and let the dough rest, covered, for 20 minutes. Knead the dough until it is smooth, 6 to 8 minutes. Add more unbleached all-purpose flour as needed to prevent the dough from sticking to your hands or the counter. Place the dough in a large vegetable shortening greased bowl, turning the dough to coat all sides with grease. Cover the bowl with a damp towel and let rise until double, about 2 hours.

4. Punch the dough down, shape it into two loaves (see directions for Popcorn White Loaf, page 90), and place the loaves in vegetable shortening greased 9 × 5-inch loaf pans. Cover the loaves and let them rise again, until almost double in bulk, 60 to 75 minutes. Bake at 325°F for 40 to 50 minutes, or until hollow sounding when knocked on the bottom. Cool on wire racks before slicing.

Hominy-Leek Monkey Bread

I often marvel at how inventive monkeys are. I mean, *wow*, this pull-apart bread is one of my favorite soup companions. The hominy in the dough acts much the way that mashed potatoes act in some breads, making for a moist and mild bread. The leeks flavor the bread just enough, and make the bread smell heavenly.

You'll have some hominy left over from the can you open. My mother discovered that hominy works fabulously in stir fries, soaking up flavor and becoming firmer as it cooks.

½ cup canned hominy, drained
2 tablespoons lukewarm milk (110°F), plus
   ½ cup cold milk
1⅛ teaspoons active dry or instant yeast
4 tablespoons (½ stick) unsalted butter, melted
1 tablespoon honey
½ teaspoon salt
2 cups unbleached all-purpose flour
¼ cup finely minced leek (white and light green
   parts only)
2 teaspoons finely minced fresh basil or thyme

1.   First, rice the hominy in a ricer, food mill, or food processor. You want a fine consistency ideally, but I've found that a few larger pieces won't hurt the bread. Combine the 2 tablespoons milk and the yeast in a medium bowl. To the yeast mixture, add the hominy, the ½ cup milk, 2 tablespoons

of the melted butter, the honey, and salt. Stir well, then add 1 cup flour and stir until smooth. Add another ½ cup flour and continue stirring until the flour is incorporated. Then turn the dough out onto a floured work surface and knead, adding flour as needed to keep the dough from being too sticky to handle. You'll probably add another ¼ to ½ cup flour.

2. After you've kneaded for about 5 minutes, when the dough just starts to become very smooth, add the leek and herbs, and continue kneading just until they're distributed throughout the dough. Place the dough in a vegetable shortening greased bowl, turning the dough to coat it with grease; cover the bowl and let rise in a warm place until doubled in size, 75 to 90 minutes.

3. Turn the dough out onto the floured work surface again and knead it briefly just to knock the air out. Pinch off a bit of dough and round it between your palms to make a golf ball–size, well, ball. Dip the ball halfway into the remaining 2 tablespoons of melted butter and place it in a buttered 8½- or 9-inch ring mold. Fill up the ring mold with two layers of these balls, packed snugly against each other. (If you don't have a ring mold, a 9 × 5-inch loaf pan will do nicely.) Cover the bread and let it rise a final time until nice and puffy, 30 to 40 minutes. During the final rise, preheat your oven to 450°F. Bake the bread for 20 to 30 minutes, until nicely browned. Serve hot.

Popcorn Pita Bread

If you've never had freshly baked pita bread, do yourself a favor and make this recipe as soon as possible. It's really no more trouble than any other yeast bread, and the combination of popcorn flour and whole wheat flour makes for an earthy and inviting pita. Most of the pitas you can buy taste like cardboard compared to these.

> One ¼-ounce packet or 2¼ teaspoons active dry
>   or instant yeast
> 1 tablespoon olive oil
> 1 teaspoon salt
> ¼ teaspoon sugar
> 1 cup whole wheat flour
> 1½ cups unbleached all-purpose flour
> 1½ cups popcorn flour (page 22)

1. Let the yeast dissolve in 1⅓ cups lukewarm (110°F) water. Stir in all the other ingredients, except that you should add only ½ cup of the whole wheat flour and 1 cup of the all-purpose flour. Beat the mixture until it is smooth, then stir in the remaining ½ cup whole wheat flour and ½ cup all-purpose flour.

2. Turn the dough out onto a floured work surface and knead until smooth and elastic, about 5 minutes, adding flour only to combat stickiness. Put the kneaded dough into a medium bowl that has been greased with olive oil, cover the

bowl, and let the dough rise in a warm place until doubled in bulk, 1 hour or more.

3. Punch the dough down and divide it into 6 equal pieces. Shape each piece into a ball, then put the balls on a baking sheet, cover them, and let them rise until puffy, about 30 minutes. On a well-floured work surface roll each ball to a thickness of about ⅛ inch. Don't worry about making each pita perfectly round. Sprinkle cornmeal on 3 baking sheets, then place 2 pitas on each sheet, cover, and let rise a final time, about 30 minutes. While they're rising, preheat your oven to 450°F.

4. Bake the pitas, one sheet at a time, for 8 to 10 minutes, until they're puffed up and slightly brown. Don't fret if your pita doesn't "balloon." When you take the pitas from the oven, wrap them together in a kitchen towel until you're ready to serve them.

Nineteenth-Century Thirded Bread

makes 1 loaf

This loaf is a modern take on the many nineteenth-century American breads that combined cornmeal, rye flour, and wheat flour. The use of cornmeal and rye flour helped stretch the precious supply of wheat flour, but also added bold flavors. This bread is a crusty and hearty rustic loaf that's a suitable partner for roasts, soups, and stews.

> One ¼-ounce packet or 2¼ teaspoons active dry
>   or instant yeast
> 1 teaspoon sugar
> 1 teaspoon salt
> 2 tablespoons unsalted butter, softened
> ⅔ cup corn flour
> ⅔ cup rye flour
> ¾ cup unbleached all-purpose flour, plus more
>   as needed

1. Let the yeast dissolve in 1 cup of lukewarm (110°F) water in a large bowl. Stir in the sugar, salt, and butter. Add the corn flour and rye flour and stir until smooth. Slowly add ¾ cup of the all-purpose flour while stirring, then turn the dough out onto a floured work surface and knead for 10 minutes, adding flour as necessary to keep it from sticking to your hands or the work surface. The dough will become smooth and elastic. Place the dough in a vegetable shortening greased bowl, turning it to coat with grease, then cover and let rise in a warm

place until doubled in size, 1 to 1½ hours. Punch the dough down and let it rest 5 minutes.

2. Shape the dough into an oval loaf by first forming a round loaf and then squeezing and tapering its ends. Slash the loaf diagonally a few times with a very sharp knife or razor blade. Sprinkle the loaf liberally with flour, cover, and let it rise again until it is nicely enlarged and puffy, 45 minutes or more. While it is rising, preheat your baking stone at 425°F on the bottom shelf of your oven. Below and to the side of your baking stone, place an empty loaf pan or small baking pan.

3. When the loaf is ready, quickly slide it onto the hot baking stone, then toss 1 cup of cold water with 2 ice cubes in it into the empty pan to create steam. Do all this as quickly as possible. Bake the loaf for 30 minutes, then lower the oven temperature to 375°F and bake another 10 to 20 minutes, until the loaf is crusty and hollow sounding when tapped on the bottom.

Honey Snail

I love the possibilities of this soft and sweet breakfast bread: it can be sliced, pulled apart, torn, slathered with butter, dunked in coffee, piled with applesauce, eaten by hand, eaten with silverware, eaten cold, eaten hot, featured as the star of a breakfast, relegated to a supporting role in a grand brunch, made to seem glamorous, made to seem common. It's pure breakfast anarchy. But the best part is the sweet honey goo that sticks to the underside of the snail. You could also use this dough to make cinnamon rolls.

1⅛ teaspoons active dry or instant yeast

2 large egg yolks

3 tablespoons quick oats

3 tablespoons unsalted butter, softened

2 tablespoons packed brown sugar

¾ teaspoon salt

1 cup unbleached all-purpose flour,
    plus more as needed

½ cup currants

¼ cup corn flour

TOPPING

¼ cup granulated sugar

¼ cup sliced almonds

¼ cup honey

2 tablespoons milk

2 tablespoons unsalted butter

1. Let the yeast dissolve in ½ cup lukewarm (110°F) water in a medium bowl. Add the egg yolks, oats, butter, sugar, and salt and whisk well. Add half of the flour and whisk the mixture until it is smooth. Stir in the remaining flour, the currants, and the corn flour. Stir until everything is well combined.

2. Turn the dough out onto a floured work surface and knead it until it is smooth and elastic, about 5 minutes. Yes, the dough will be very wet at this point, and a bit tricky to handle, but don't be afraid to keep adding flour to prevent it from sticking. It will probably take another ¼ cup of flour while you knead it.

3. In a covered and vegetable shortening greased bowl, let the dough rise in a warm place until nearly doubled in size, 75 to 90 minutes. After an hour or more, when the dough is approaching its doubling point, prepare the topping. In a small saucepan, combine all the topping ingredients and stir over medium heat until the mixture begins bubbling and frothing. Remove the pan from the heat while you prepare the dough for the second rising.

4. Turn the dough back out onto the work surface and roll it into a 4½-foot-long rope. Coil this rope into a vegetable shortening greased 9-inch pie pan. Arrange the coil so that it doesn't touch itself, i.e., has a big gap between its own coils. Pour the still warm topping all over the coil. Yes, some of it will coat the coil itself, but most of the topping will pool in the bottom of the pie plate. That's the idea! Gently cover the coil with plastic wrap and allow it to rise again until it's puffy and has closed up all its gaps 20 to 30 minutes. Meanwhile, preheat the oven to 375°F. Bake the snail for 22 to 26 minutes, until it's browned on the top and bottom and hollow sounding when tapped.

Yeast Cornbreads

Anadama Batter Bread

makes 1 loaf

I have never in my life seen a cookbook without anadama bread in it. Even the famous *No Anadama Bread in this Cookbook Cookbook* had no less than *seven* variations on this classic American bread. The most annoying thing of all is that every cookbook prints the little backstory to the bread (which, by the way, is based only on hearsay). The short version:

1. Long ago, wife cooks same cornmeal mush and molasses for dinner every night.
2. Husband, a fisherman, tires of routine.
3. Finally husband snaps on coming home to the same meal, and utters the following:
4. "God damn that god damn Anna and her god damn mush and god damn molasses every god damn night."
5. He mixes the mush and molasses with some flour and bakes it.
6. It's not half bad.
7. He's invented a new bread.
8. In the course of a messy divorce, Anna wins the copyright to the famous recipe.
9. History shortens the husband's rant to "Anna, damn her," which for some unknown reason is shortened further, then misspelled, and becomes the name of the bread he supposedly invented.

In the spirit of Anna's alleged laziness, I present this bread as a batter bread, which means you don't have to knead it, dammit.

⅓ cup cornmeal

¼ cup molasses

2 tablespoons unsalted butter, cut into small pieces

1 teaspoon salt

One ¼-ounce packet or 2¼ teaspoons active dry or
    instant yeast

1 large egg

2½ cups unbleached all-purpose flour

Cornmeal and salt for topping

1.   Pour ¾ cup boiling water over the cornmeal and stir. Add the molasses, butter, and salt. Stir until the butter is melted. Separately dissolve the yeast in ¼ cup lukewarm water (110°F) and then add it to the cornmeal mixture. Add the egg and half of the flour and beat the mixture with a hand mixer at medium speed (or whisk by hand) for 2 or 3 minutes. Add the remaining flour and stir until the batter is smooth.

2.   Spread the batter into a vegetable shortening greased medium loaf pan and pat the top smooth with floured fingers. Sprinkle the top of the loaf with cornmeal and salt, cover it, and let it rise in a warm place until it is a bit more than doubled in bulk, 60 to 90 minutes. Near the end of the rising, preheat your oven to 350°F. Bake the bread for 50 to 70 minutes—covering the top of the bread with aluminum foil after 20 minutes—until firm and hollow sounding when tapped on the bottom. Remove the loaf from its pan and let it cool on a wire rack.

Gospel Buns

These diminutive buns are cousins to English muffins. They're soft and pillowy and lovely when warm. I like them at breakfast, but they also make dainty little sandwich buns—for a teahouse kind of lunch, for example. Or you can make them slightly larger and thicker so that they are normal-size sandwich buns.

1 cup milk

4 tablespoons (½ stick) unsalted butter

One ¼-ounce packet or 2¼ teaspoons active dry
   or instant yeast

2 cups (approximately) unbleached all-purpose flour

½ cup corn flour

2 teaspoons sugar

1 teaspoon salt

1. In a saucepan or microwave (on low power), gently heat the milk and butter until the milk is lukewarm (110°F) and the butter is melted. Pour the milk into a medium bowl, add the yeast, and let it dissolve. Add the remaining ingredients, except that you should add only 1½ cups of the all-purpose flour. Stir the mixture vigorously for a minute, then slowly stir in the final ½ cup of flour—or as much flour as it takes to make a soft dough.

2. Turn the dough out onto a floured work surface and knead it until it is smooth and elastic, about 5 minutes, adding just enough all-purpose flour to keep the dough from

sticking to your hands or the counter. Form the kneaded dough into a ball, coat the dough with flour, and let it rise in a vegetable shortening greased bowl in a warm place until doubled in size, 50 to 70 minutes. Punch the dough down, then let it rise a second time until almost doubled in bulk, 45 to 60 minutes.

3.　Near the end of the second rising, preheat your oven to 375°F and sprinkle a baking sheet liberally with cornmeal. Turn the dough out onto a well-floured surface and gently roll the dough to a thickness of ½ inch or more. Cut the dough into squares (I like 3-inch squares) with a pizza cutter. Place the squares on the baking sheet and sprinkle them with cornmeal, then bake for 8 minutes. Flip the buns and bake them for another 6 to 12 minutes, until they're lightly browned.

Soft Corn Rolls

makes 20 to 30 rolls

I love the texture and slight sweetness of these dinner rolls.

One ¼-ounce packet or 2¼ teaspoons active dry or
  instant yeast
½ cup lukewarm milk (110°F)
3¼ cups unbleached all-purpose flour
1 cup canned cream-style corn
1 large egg
¼ cup canola oil
2 tablespoons sugar
¾ teaspoon salt

1. Dissolve the yeast in the warm milk. Then add 1½ cups of the flour and all the remaining ingredients. Stir the mixture vigorously until it is smooth, then go ahead and stir it a bit more. Now stir in the remaining 1¾ cups of flour in two or three additions, or as much flour as it takes to make a soft but kneadable dough.

2. Turn the dough out onto a floured work surface and let it rest for 5 to 10 minutes. Knead the dough until it is smooth and elastic, about 5 minutes, adding more flour if necessary. Round the dough up and place it in a vegetable shortening greased bowl, rotating the dough in the bowl to grease it, too. Cover the bowl and let the dough rise in a warm place until it's doubled in size, 60 to 80 minutes. Punch the dough down, turn it over, and let it rise again until nearly double, 25 to 30 minutes.

3. Turn the dough back out onto the floured work surface and knead it tenderly for 15 seconds—just to knock the air out. Cover the dough with a towel and let it rest 5 minutes. Now shape the dough into whatever roll shape you want. I like a classic round roll. I fit 13 balls of dough—somewhere between a golf ball and a tennis ball in size—in a greased 9-inch round cake pan. This recipe makes two pans. But other roll shapes will work just as well.

4. Cover the shaped rolls and allow them to rise a final time, until they puff up nicely, 15 to 25 minutes. Meanwhile, preheat your oven to 425°F. Bake the rolls for 12 to 18 minutes.

Popcorn Focaccia

makes 2 small-medium pizzas or focaccias

Who do I think I am? How did I come up with such an idea? Isn't it illegal to put popcorn in anything Italian? Is this perhaps the best recipe in the entire book? If this focaccia fought a normal focaccia, which would win? (This one.) Why aren't there more flatbreads in your life? When are you going to make this? How do those wonderfully big bubbles get into the dough? Who do I think I am?

This focaccia also makes my favorite pizza dough. The only change you might want to make is to reduce the salt to 1 teaspoon or 1¼ teaspoons. A baking stone makes for a crusty bread. This bread freezes well—cut it into sticks before freezing and then pop them in the toaster oven when you need them.

One ¼-ounce packet or 2½ teaspoons active dry
    or instant yeast
2½ cups unbleached all-purpose flour,
    plus more as needed
1 cup popcorn flour (page 22)
2 tablespoons olive oil, plus more for bowl
1½ teaspoons salt

1. Allow the yeast to dissolve in 1¼ cups lukewarm water (110°F) in a mixing bowl. Add 2 cups of the all-purpose flour, the popcorn flour, oil, and salt, and stir vigorously for 3 minutes. Now stir in the remaining ½ cup flour, just until you have a soft but kneadable dough. My dough usually takes a total of 2½ cups flour in the bowl, plus another ¼ cup while kneading.

2. Turn the dough out onto a floured work surface and knead it until it is smooth and elastic, about 5 minutes, adding only as much flour as is needed to keep it from sticking to your hands and counter. Drizzle olive oil into a medium bowl and then turn the dough in the bowl to coat it with oil. Let the dough rise, covered, until doubled in size, 60 minutes or more. Punch the dough down, turn it over, cover it, and let it rise again until doubled, 30 to 45 minutes.

3. Divide the dough into two equal pieces and put each piece onto a cornmeal-sprinkled pizza peel, largish cutting board, or the backside of a baking sheet (the idea is that the focaccia needs to be able to easily slide off onto the baking stone). Gently poke each piece of dough with the tips of your fingers to flatten it a bit and press some of the air out. At this point, preheat your baking stone in your oven at 450°F. Let the dough rest 10 minutes.

4. Now shape the dough into two rough rectangles (this is a rustic bread—it shouldn't be perfectly shaped) by poking at it with your fingertips and tugging gently if necessary. The end product should be about ½ inch thick. Slash the top of each focaccia with 4 or 6 slashes in a grid pattern, but only if you have a very sharp knife or razor blade—a dull knife will tear the fragile dough. Cover the dough and let it rise a final time, until puffy, 30 minutes or so.

5. In one swift motion, slide one focaccia onto the hot baking stone and bake for 10 to 15 minutes, until lightly browned, stiff, and hollow sounding when tapped on the bottom. Then bake the second focaccia.

6. Serve warm, sliced in long narrow breadsticks.

Additions: The focaccia is so fantastic by itself, as an accompaniment to anything Italian, that I never dress it up. Nonetheless, some common additions and/or toppings for focaccia include olives, thyme, sage, oregano, olive oil, rosemary, coarse salt, pepper, parsley, Parmesan cheese, onion, etc. You can knead small amounts of these ingredients into the dough and also sprinkle them on top.

LEFTOVER CORNBREADS

In which cornbread, in its closing act, proves its usefulness and versatility even after its freshest hour has passed.

Here's a soup and a salad, as well as Cornbread Dressing. Witness, too, the many uses of Toasted Cornbread Crumbles.

Cornbread Dressing

I admit that this is the one recipe I swiped directly from my mother. Living in Missouri, a border state, we referred to it as both stuffing, like northerners, and dressing, like southerners. In my family, dressing is perhaps the most requested dish. Often Mom would put small bits of already baked chicken or turkey into the dressing, making it almost a one-dish meal. As with any dressing, getting the right moisture level can be tricky. Some people like a dry dressing, while others like a soggy one. Experiment to find what works for you.

5 cups crumbled or grated cornbread
   (fresh or frozen)
3 cups grated white bread
   (frozen is easier to grate)
½ cup diced celery
½ cup diced onion
⅓ cup (5⅓ tablespoons) unsalted butter
¼ teaspoon sage
¼ teaspoon thyme
¼ teaspoon savory
Pinch of freshly ground black pepper
1 cup chicken broth

1.   Preheat your oven to 375°F.

2.   Put the grated cornbread and white bread into a large bowl and set aside.

116   The Cornbread Book

3. Sauté the celery and onion in the butter until they are tender. Add the sage, thyme, savory, and pepper and let them heat in the skillet for a minute or so.

4. Stir the celery/onion mixture into the bread mixture. Then drizzle in the chicken broth, stirring.

5. Pour the dressing into a 9 × 12-inch baking dish and press it down very lightly with a spatula. Bake for 30 to 40 minutes, until toasted looking and slightly dry on top.

Buttermilk Cornbread Soup

This inventive soup is from Betty Fussell's remarkable book *Crazy for Corn*. She points out that the soup includes cornbread, buttermilk, and collard greens, which "are a kind of Deep South Trinity."

4 cups crumbled cornbread
5 cups buttermilk
½ small onion, finely chopped
1 cup finely shredded cooked collards or other greens
½ small hot red or green chile pepper, minced
1½ teaspoons bacon or ham fat or vegetable oil
1 to 2 cups regular milk
Salt and freshly ground black pepper

1. Puree the cornbread and buttermilk together in two batches in a food processor to make as smooth as possible. Pour the mixture into a saucepan and bring to a simmer. Remove from the stove and cover with a lid to keep it hot.

2. In a skillet, sauté the onion, collards, and chile in the fat for 4 to 5 minutes until well mixed.

3. Reheat the soup if needed (you may need to add some regular milk to thin it, for the mixture will thicken as it stands). Season with salt and pepper, ladle into individual soup bowls, and garnish with the collard mixture.

Southern Cornbread Salad

serves 8 to 12

This lively and colorful dish is commonly sighted at potlucks in the South and Midwest. How can anything with a whole cup of mayonnaise and nine slices of bacon taste bad?

1 recipe of cornbread, cooled, crumbled

THE "VEGETABLE" LAYER
4 tomatoes, chopped
1 green pepper, diced
1 onion, diced
1 cup of sweet pickles, diced
9 slices of bacon, cooked and crumbled

THE DRESSING
1 cup mayonnaise
¼ cup sweet pickle juice
2 tablespoons sugar

1. Stir together the "vegetables" (yes, that includes the bacon). Separately combine the dressing ingredients until smooth.

2. Assemble the salad in a large salad bowl by layering it in this order (starting at the bottom): half of the cornbread, half of the vegetables, half of the dressing. Repeat.

A Grab Bag of **OTHER USES** for Cornbread

- *A traditional southern treat is to crumble cornbread into a glass of cold buttermilk, or sprinkle it into a bowl of buttermilk and eat it like soup.*

- *Make an excellent bread pudding by substituting crumbled or cubed cornbread for about 25 percent of the bread in any bread pudding recipe.*

- *One of the most versatile uses for leftover cornbread is what I call Toasted Cornbread Crumbles. Finely grate your cornbread (frozen cornbread grates more uniformly), then spread the crumbs on a baking sheet and toast them lightly in the oven, just until they start to brown. Then you can sprinkle the Crumbles on your morning yogurt, or your midnight bowl of ice cream. The Crumbles also jazz up salads nicely, or serve as a crunchy topping for a casserole. Add Crumbles to granola, make a pudding with them, or put them on hot macaroni and cheese. Keep your Crumbles in an airtight container in the freezer and they'll last for months.*

- *Make croutons with cornbread by cubing it, then either baking or sautéing the cubes in a bit of oil. Add salt and herbs to taste.*

The Cornbread Book

SOURCES

King Arthur Flour/The Baker's Catalogue
P. O. Box 876
Norwich, VT 05055
800-827-6836
www.bakerscatalogue.com
Sells a whole-grain organic cornmeal, in addition to a dizzying array of top-notch wheat flours and baking supplies.

Bob's Red Mill Natural Foods
5209 SE International Way
Milwaukie, OR 97222
800-349-2173
www.bobsredmill.com
Found in many supermarkets, their whole-grain cornmeal and corn flour can be bought online and via mail order.

Nora Mill Granary
7107 South Main St.
Helen, GA 30545
www.noramill.com
Locally grown corn and other grains are stone-ground in this 125-year-old water-powered mill.

War Eagle Mill
11045 War Eagle Rd.
Rogers, AR 72756
479-789-5343
www.wareaglemill.com
A water-powered mill built in 1973 on the site of three previous mills, War Eagle Mill produces organic whole-grain cornmeals, as well as many other products.

Weisenberger Mill
P. O. Box 215
Midway, KY 40347
859-254-5282 or
800-643-8678
www.weisenberger.com
This water-powered mill has been operated by the same family for six generations. It mills not only very good whole-grain cornmeals but also flours, grits, and mixes.

www.glutenfreemall.com
Sell's Authentic Foods corn flour, as well as a couple of kinds of cornmeal.

www.nationalcornbread.com
Home of the National Cornbread Festival, held the last weekend of April each year in South Pittsburg, Tennessee. Cornbread cookoffs, a carnival, music, arts and crafts, antique tractors, a 5-k road race, and more! Sponsored by Lodge Manufacturing, maker of the indispensable cast iron cookware that we cornbread cooks can't live without.

BIBLIOGRAPHY

Betty Crocker's Picture Cook Book. Minneapolis: General Mills, Inc., 1950.

Billings, Josh. *Everybody's Friend, or; Josh Billings's Encyclopedia and Proverbial Philosophy of Wit and Humor.* Hartford: American Publishing Co., 1874.

Child, Lydia. *The American Frugal Housewife,* 16th ed. Boston: Carter, Hendee, and Co., 1835.

Davidson, Alan. *The Oxford Companion to Food.* New York: Oxford University Press, 1999.

Fussell, Betty. *Crazy for Corn.* New York: HarperPerennial, 1995.

——. *The Story of Corn.* New York: Alfred A. Knopf, 1992.

Giles, Dorothy. *Singing Valleys: The Story of Corn.* New York: Random House, 1940.

Hardeman, Nicholas P. *Shucks, Shocks, and Hominy Blocks: Corn as a Way of Life in Pioneer America.* Baton Rouge and London: Louisiana State University Press, 1981.

Hariot, Thomas. *A Brief and True Report of the New Found Land of Virginia.* Facsimile of 1588 ed. New York: Dodd, Mead, and Co., 1903.

Hess, John L., and Karen Hess. *The Taste of America*. New York: Grossman Publishers, 1977.

Hunt, Caroline, and C. F. Langworthy. "Corn Meal as a Food and Ways of Using It." Farmer's bulletin 565, United States Department of Agriculture, 1917.

Jackson, Jeremy. *Life at These Speeds*. New York: Thomas Dunne Books, 2002.

Murphy, Charles J. *American Indian Corn (Maize): A Cheap, Wholesome, and Nutritious Food, 150 Ways to Prepare and Cook It.* New York and London: G. P. Putnam's Sons, 1917.

Simmons, Amelia. *American Cookery* (1796). Facsimile ed: Ed. M. T. Wilson. New York: Oxford University Press, 1958.

Smith, Andrew F. *A Social History of Popcorn in America.* Columbia, S.C.: University of South Carolina Press, 1999.

Thoreau, Henry David. *Walden; or, Life in the Woods*. Boston: Ticknor and Fields, 1854.

The Cornbread Song

Lyrics and music by Jeremy Jackson © 2003

CHORUS
```
C    G       C    F        C
```
Cornbread in the morning, cornbread at noon,
```
       G         Am        F        C G C
```
and in the afternoon, I had cornbread, and at supper, too.

```
   G              C           F                 C
```
Some people like their cornbread yellow, some people like it white,
```
   G           Am          F          C G C
```
but I'm here to say that it's good both ways, so let's not fight.

CHORUS

```
       G        C        F                    C
```
Did you ever see a rooster smile as he watched the rising sun?
```
      G         Am              F          C G C
```
That is how I feel as my cornbread bakes and it's almost done.

CHORUS

```
F        C      Am                  Em      F
```
Cornbread, cornbread—every night I dream of cornbread
```
        C       Em               G7          C
```
Cornbread, cornbread—how I long to eat your steamy center, uh huh

INSTRUMENTAL: G Am Em F C F G
```
C              G      Am        Em   F
```
Cornbread in the morning, cornbread at noon,
```
            C     F                G
```
cornbread in the afternoon, and at supper, too.

CGAmEmFCFGC
la di da di da, la di da di da, la dah dah dah dah duh, uh uh, uh uh,
uh huh . . .

INDEX

strawberries, 38
stuffing, cornbread, 116–17
sugar, brown, 39
summer kitchen pound cake,
    86–87
sunflower seed cornbread, 46
sweet cornbread, 30–31
sweet potato cupcakes,
    82–83
syrup, maple, 39

tamale pie, 55
thirded bread, 13–14
    nineteenth-century, 102–3
tomatoes, sun-dried, 38
toppings:
    for choco-corno-espresso-
        almondo biscotti, 78–80
    dumpling, 44–45
    for honey snail, 104–5
    for persimmon coffee cake,
        76–77

uppity cornmeal crepes:
    dessert, 57
    dinner, 56–57

velvet spoonbread, 52–53

waffles, cornmeal, 51
walnuts, 38
wheat flour, 7–9, 12–15
wheat germ, toasted:
    in caramel corncake, 81
    in cornmeal waffles, 51

yeast, 12, 13–14, 24
    cornbreads, 89–114
yogurt, 39
    in healthier cornbread, 37
    in summer kitchen pound
        cake, 86–87

zaletti, 74–75
Zuni bread, new, 96–97